THE Highway Called Life

Driving in Search of Meaning

Jaskiran Arora

BlueRose ONE.com
Stories Matter
New Delhi • London

BLUEROSE PUBLISHERS
India | U.K.

BlueRose ONE.com
Stories Matter
NewDelhi • London

For permissions requests or inquiries regarding this publication, please contact:

BLUEROSE PUBLISHERS
www.BlueRoseONE.com
info@bluerosepublishers.com
+91 8882 898 898
+4407342408967

ISBN: 978-93-7139-530-4

Cover design: Yash Singhal
Typesetting: Namrata Saini

First Edition: September 2025

Preface

This book was conceptualised during my many long, quiet drives on the highway. In those in-between moments, when the world outside the window blurred into motion, thoughts turned into metaphors, and metaphors into meaning.

This book is not a manual. It won't tell you how to drive, how fast to go, or which exit to take.

Instead, it offers a series of conversations, reflections, and metaphors - drawn from ordinary moments made extraordinary by presence.

While Sagar and Riddhi are fictional, their conversations echo the fleeting thoughts that visit us all, quiet reflections we often feel but rarely voice. Thoughts that emerge on foggy mornings, while waiting at traffic lights, or winding down a quiet road during a long drive. I believe a little bit of both Sagar and Riddhi live in all of us, in our wonder, our weariness, and despite, in our will to keep moving.

I hope this book helps you feel a little more understood, and maybe even lends greater meaning to your own journey. Because life, after all, is a drive.

Thank you for riding along.

Warmly,

Jaskiran Arora

Dedication

To my Papa, my first co-passenger!

Because of you, Papa, I learned how to be.

I exist because of you.

This book exists because of you.

Every page carries your quiet strength,

and the echo of the hand that never let go...

Contents

Acknowledgements

This book is not mine alone. It is a thread in the collage of lives, moments, pauses, and people that have shaped me, gently and powerfully, over time.

First and foremost, I offer my deepest gratitude to the Universe for conspiring through moments of quiet, detours, and divine interruptions to bring this book into being. For the grace that arrived in whispers, through a long drive, a fleeting thought, a paused traffic light, or a sudden stillness, and wove itself into words. This book happened not because I planned it, but because life nudged me toward it, again and again, until I could no longer ignore its call.

To my family, who graciously did without me on many cozy afternoons, while I sat lost in metaphor, chasing meaning across pages. Thank you for your patience, for your quiet understanding, and for offering the green signal of encouragement after reading just the first chapter. Your warmth has always been the wind beneath every word I write.

To my friends and to my students, who, over the years, have become friends, for being my mirrors, cheerleaders, and co-creators of meaning: thank you. For believing in me when I doubted myself, for holding up gentle criticism like a compass, and for reminding me that authenticity is always more powerful than perfection. Your presence has shaped both the silences and the sentences of this book.

To BML Munjal University (BMU), my heartfelt thanks for the trust placed in me and for providing the space, opportunities, and encouragement to dream, to envision, and to discover my own soul print. Your faith has been both an anchor and a springboard, allowing my personal and creative journey to unfold with courage and clarity.

I would also like to express my deepest gratitude to SKC World for being a powerful catalyst in my journey of inner transformation. The frameworks, guidance, and immersive experiences shared through SKC gently but firmly shifted my perspective from chasing external validation to embracing internal alignment.

And lastly, to you, dear reader - thank you for being here. For walking beside me through these pages. For being a co-traveller on this journey called life. May the metaphors linger long after the drive ends.

With love, grace, and quiet joy,

Jaskiran

Chapter 1

The Long Drive

"Some roads are meant to be savoured. Not sprinted."

The alarm buzzed.

7:00 a.m.

Sagar groaned, eyes heavy with sleep, his limbs unwilling to move. But then he remembered Riddhi's message from last night, *"No backing out this time. Long drive. Tomorrow. Non-negotiable!"*, and a lazy smile tugged at his lips as he reluctantly pulled off the quilt and quickly got ready.

He locked the door of his flat on the 9th floor and gave one last glance to ensure everything was in order. Getting into the lift, he caught his reflection in the mirror and paused for a moment. The black jacket suited him, understated, well-fitted, effortlessly confident. At a little over 5 feet 8 inches, Sagar carried himself with the quiet assurance of someone who didn't need to raise his voice to be heard. His square jaw was freshly shaved, adding a sharpness to his features, but it was his eyes that held attention, deep, probing, the kind that seemed to listen even when he didn't speak. He tilted his head slightly, adjusted his collar, and gave a faint, approving nod. Not bad, he thought. Not bad at all.

Stepping out of the lift, he saw the security guard standing up and saluting him in respect and admiration. After all, Sagar always addressed the guard by his first name and never failed to enquire about his well-being. Today was no different. Sagar smiled back and gave him a casual salute, checking if all was well.

Walking towards his car, humming, he unlocked his cave-black Urban Cruiser parked in the last spot in the society's parking lot, in Gurgaon. It was a perfect day for the long drive he had agreed to with Riddhi the previous evening.

A light chill hung in the air, a quiet prelude to the brutal North Indian winter that would soon settle over the high-rises, posh colonies, and buzzing streets of Gurgaon. The kind of cold that creeps in slowly… and then stays.

Adjusting his glasses and unzipping his leather jacket, he stepped into the car. Ah, he loved that new-car fragrance; it still lingered from when he had bought it just last month after he received a huge bonus for his exceptional performance.

The IT industry was competitive, fiercely so. But for someone with a razor-sharp analytical mind and a knack for seeing the bigger picture, it was a space to thrive. And Sagar did more than just thrive; he stood out.

In his role as Director- Business Development, he had the rare ability to decode what the client truly needed, craft a seamless execution plan, and present it with such clarity and charm that the deal rarely slipped away. He didn't just win business, he won trust. He was the kind of team member every boss hoped for. With Sagar on board, targets weren't just met, they were consistently outdone.

He adjusted the rearview mirror and checked the sideview mirrors. All was well. He glanced at the clock on the dashboard.

7:30 a.m.

He realized he needed to hurry. Riddhi, his colleague, his carpool partner, and more importantly, his best friend since kindergarten, was probably already waiting. He had better get moving.

Sagar leaned back into the driver's seat, settling into the rhythm of the road. Riddhi's house was just 500 metres away. He pulled up in front of her building and called to let her know he had arrived.

She appeared in no time, wearing a white *kurti* with a delicate floral print and well-fitted blue jeans. Just 5 feet 2 inches, Riddhi had a presence that felt larger than her frame, radiant and warm.

She was a senior leader in the Communications department, a space where words build trust and alignment. Her role went beyond crafting messages; it was about understanding the organization's purpose, sensing how words would land, and creating a connection. With a sharp mind and a deeply empathetic core, she knew how to listen, distil, and deliver with impact.

Her fair complexion glowed softly in the morning light, and her shoulder-length dark brown hair framed her face in gentle waves. A small, graceful nose sat perfectly above lips that seemed always poised between a smile and a secret, full, expressive, and effortlessly kind.

A pair of diamond-studded earrings gleamed playfully as she approached, catching the sunlight with each step. But what truly made her unforgettable was the expression she wore, a smile that lived not only on her lips, but in her eyes, deep and soulful, as if they saw right through to the heart of whoever looked into them.

Behind her, the *kachnar* trees in the garden were in full bloom with purple flowers- a magnificent sight, though somehow, she outshone even that. As she stepped into the car and pulled the seatbelt across, the mild floral fragrance of her perfume enveloped Sagar.

Click. She fastened the seatbelt and smiled.

"Good morning, Mr. Sagar Sachdeva! How are you doing this morning?"

"Couldn't be better! All thanks to you and your 'stupid' idea of this long drive, Ms. Riddhi Kalra! Imagine waking up at 7:00 a.m. on a Sunday! Who does that?" Sagar faked grumbling.

"Haha, very funny! Is 7:00 a.m. early? Really?" she laughed mockingly, gazing out the window and soaking in the morning sun.

"I promise you, the spot I'm taking you to today is worth a hundred early Sunday mornings you'll willingly sacrifice. The scenery is magnificent." Riddhi said dreamily.

"Well, it better be!" Sagar said, playfully threatening her.

Once they were comfortably settled, Sagar played their favourite Kishore Da playlist and steered the car out of the city's concrete chaos and onto the open highway. The mustard fields skirted the road, and the sky melted into golden hues, divinity in motion.

Riddhi tapped her fingers to the beat of the music, her head tilted, eyes closed, just listening. Leaning back, one foot tucked under her leg, she said,

"You know… this is nice. No meetings. No deadlines. No clients shouting, 'This is urgent!' Just us, this music, this breeze, these views, and" she stopped mid-sentence, the words suddenly too fragile to carry.

"And…?" he nudged gently, his voice teasing, but his gaze soft, lingering a moment longer than it needed to, as her *kurti* flapped in the wind.

She gave a quick, dismissive laugh, turning her face toward the window.

"Nothing," she replied. A little too quickly. A little too lightly.

But inside, she felt it, how her heart always settled around him. There was something about Sagar's presence- his steadiness, his quiet way of noticing things without making a fuss - that made her feel like the world could be kind after all.

They had known each other forever, or at least, that's what it felt like. From scraped knees to school picnics and teenage heartbreaks, Sagar had always been there. Protective, caring, dependable.

But then again, he was like that with everyone. Riddhi had often reminded herself of that: he wasn't doing anything special for her.

During their teenage years, they would laugh and confide in each other about their latest crushes, his on a senior basketball player, hers on a boy who played the drums. It was easy, uncomplicated. Platonic love, pure and simple.

Later, as young adults, both had been in serious relationships with different people. Yet, no matter how committed they were, neither ever found the quiet ease and emotional shorthand they had with each other.

With Sagar, words were almost optional, because even the silences between them spoke. Feelings didn't need loud declarations; they existed in shared glances, in knowing smiles, in the comfort of just being.

It wasn't love; she told herself. It wasn't even infatuation. Just... a strange sense of warmth. Of wanting to stay a little longer. Of not needing to explain who she was.

She had never admitted this feeling, not to herself, not to anyone. And to him? Definitely not. She didn't want to name the relationship. Not yet. Because sometimes, just sitting next to someone in silence was enough. Enough to know something was there. Even if neither of them said it out loud.

Sagar smirked. "Don't get too comfortable. You're back to being tortured tomorrow at 9 a.m.!"

"I know. Let me have this moment," she said, dramatically pulling herself out of the depths of the thought.

She turned her face slightly toward him. "And hey... thank you. For saying yes to this *mad* plan. I know you're not a morning person. Especially after yesterday's endless Saturday meetings."

He shot her a sideways smile, eyes lingering on her face a fraction longer than they should have. "You're right. I'm not a morning person at all. But... I'm glad I said yes. Though I still don't know how you convinced me to get up this early," he added, smiling again, trying to mask the quick flutter in his chest.

Because truth be told, every time he looked into her eyes, especially in moments like this, something inside him stuttered. A skipped heartbeat. A silent question. But he held it close, hidden beneath easy smiles and safe words. He wasn't sure how she felt. And he didn't want to risk turning something beautiful into something awkward. Or fragile.

Riddhi laughed, her eyes crinkling in that way that always made it harder for him to look away. She glanced at him for just a second longer, searching, maybe, for something unspoken.

But then she turned back to the road ahead, brushing a stray strand of hair behind her ear.

No words passed. And yet, the silence said just enough.

Sagar shrugged. "It's just been… a lot lately. Performance reviews, team restructuring, this new London client breathing down my neck…"

"And don't forget the award," she added, raising an eyebrow.

"What award?"

"Oh, come on," she scoffed. "The 'Leadership Excellence' thing. The LinkedIn post with 1,400 likes and a hashtag overdose? Even our high school librarian commented."

He rolled his eyes. "Just something people expect you to post. Doesn't mean much."

"Why not?" she asked. "You earned every bit of it. And you rightly deserved the big bonus and the annual raise."

Sagar didn't respond immediately. The car cruised forward, Kishore Da's velvety voice filling the silence.

Riddhi gently prompted him to take the left turn, guiding him off the wide, bustling highway onto a narrow, single-lane road that curled and climbed into the waiting arms of the Aravalli hills. The landscape shifted instantly, the hum of traffic faded, replaced by the soft rustle of leaves and the distant call of a *koel* echoing through the valley.

The morning sun, warm and unhurried, bathed the undulating hills in a soft golden hue, casting long shadows and highlighting the rough textures of ancient rocks and scattered shrubs. Wild grasses swayed gently by the roadside, brushing against the car as it inched forward. Wisps of mist still lingered in shaded corners, slowly dissolving into the day. Above them, clouds drifted like idle thoughts across the pale blue sky, as if the whole world had slowed down to breathe.

Then, whoosh.

A silver Audi tore past them out of nowhere, startling them both.

"Whoa!" Sagar blurted, tightening his grip on the wheel as he quickly manoeuvred a sharp turn ahead.

"Oh, some people drive like they own the road!" Riddhi exclaimed, her voice a mix of shock and irritation.

A rush of adrenaline hung heavy in the silence that followed as they caught their breath.

The road was growing narrower now, winding sharply with a steep, rocky drop on their right. Sagar's hands steadied on the wheel, his focus razor-sharp. The uneven surface was littered with loose pebbles, enough to make even a minor slip feel dangerous.

In the rearview mirror, Sagar noticed a black Scorpio hurtling toward them at a reckless pace. The driver was honking incessantly, seemingly in a frenzy. With a sharp bend just ahead, there was no space to safely give way. Sagar stayed focused, driving cautiously, trying to navigate the tight curve.

But the Scorpio didn't wait.

With a loud blare of the horn, it swerved abruptly, cutting them off from the left, forcing Sagar dangerously close to the gravel edge near the pit.

And then, as if that wasn't enough, the driver leaned out, hurled a curse, and flashed Sagar a middle finger before speeding off.

Riddhi's head whipped around. "Wow. That guy's carrying some serious trauma."

Sagar's jaw clenched. His grip on the wheel turned white-knuckled.

"Hey… don't," Riddhi warned.

He pressed the accelerator.

"Sagar…"

He didn't respond. She was not sure if he was even listening to her.

"What's the point? Proving to some random guy that you're not slow? Winning a race you didn't even sign up for?" she completed her thought, her voice trembling with frustration and fear, eyes locked on the blur of the road ahead.

Still no answer.

The car surged forward.

"This is just like last week," Riddhi said, her tone calm but cutting. "Kabir took credit for your idea, and you spent the next three days out-sliding everyone in that pitch."

Kabir. The kind of colleague who walked into every room like he owned it. Charismatic, impeccably dressed, fluent in boardroom speak. He wasn't necessarily the smartest, but he mastered the art of timing, of speaking just enough, nodding at the right moment, stepping in when the applause was near. He played the game well.

To the seniors, he was a natural leader - polished, confident, always pitch-ready. To his peers, he was a puzzle - equal parts charm and calculation. He rarely built the engine but always managed to sit in the driver's seat when the deal was sealed. He didn't steal credit outright; he simply blurred the lines until no one remembered where the idea had begun.

For Sagar, Kabir was both a trigger and a mirror. A reflection of everything he refused to be, and yet, couldn't fully escape. Because for all his raw intellect and hard-earned wins, Sagar still found himself chasing validation, not from Kabir, but from a world that often clapped for the loudest, not the truest.

But today, Kabir was the least of his problems.

His eyes locked on the Scorpio ahead, his foot pressing harder, jaw clenched with the quiet fury of someone trying to prove something not just to a stranger, but to himself. With one swift surge, he overtook the car, catching a glimpse of the driver fuming in the rearview mirror. A smirk crept across his face.

"And I nailed it," he said, defending his position on the Kabir incident.

"But at what cost?" Riddhi countered, arms crossed. "You lost sleep, snapped at your analyst, and skipped your mom's check-up."

His grip tightened on the steering wheel. Her words landed, but he didn't show it. Not yet.

The Audi, the first car that had overtaken them, appeared again, tauntingly ahead. Riddhi glanced at Sagar. She knew what was coming. The next chase had begun.

85... 90... 95... 100 km/hr. And then - triumph!

"Some people need to be shown," Sagar said, his voice low but charged. "Sometimes silence looks like surrender."

Riddhi exhaled slowly. She could feel it, the wall going up. Again. That quiet storm inside him: the need to stay ahead, to not be outpaced, to not be unseen.

"You see," Sagar continued, his grin widening, "it's not about winning. It's about not being the guy who gets left behind."

She didn't respond. Not immediately. There was too much she wanted to say, but not now, not when his speed was masking something far more vulnerable underneath.

As Sagar was looking in the rearview mirror at the Audi behind, a quiet satisfaction settled in his chest. The kind that came not from speed – but from being ahead. He allowed himself a fleeting moment of triumph, his fingers drumming on the steering wheel, and the corners of his mouth lifting in a small, knowing grin.

And then, something shifted.

The Audi, now just a fading speck in the distance, suddenly veered left onto a narrow, unmarked detour and disappeared. .

No indicator. No warning. Just… gone.

Sagar blinked.

He looked into the rearview mirror again. Nothing.

There was no sign of the Audi.

Sagar's smile faltered. He eased his foot off the accelerator.

The road ahead had changed. The last 25 kilometres had passed in a blur. The hills were behind them. The trees were thinning. The sun shone hotter now.

"We missed it, Sagar." Riddhi sighed.

He turned to her, confused. Her eyes avoided his.

"Funny, isn't it?" she said softly. "We win the race… but lose the view."

"That spot I wanted to show you. The lake. The sunlight on the water. The breeze through those old trees. You were too busy racing someone who wasn't even headed where we were."

The silence in the car shifted, from adrenaline to awkward realization. Sagar's grip on the wheel loosened. The road ahead stretched out emptier now. The silence that followed wasn't celebratory. It was... sobering.

He eased. Not because he meant to, but because *something inside him had.*

His face was unreadable.

100.. 95.. 90.. 85…80…75…70…65…60 km/Hr

60 km/hr, and he put the car in cruise mode.

Only a long stretch of asphalt under a blazing sun.

The haze of adrenaline was gone. And in its place was:

Realization.

About himself.

Then he exhaled. "We're all running past something. I don't even know what I'm chasing anymore. Maybe… I am just scared that if I slow down, I won't matter."

Riddhi didn't speak immediately. Her gaze softened.

"You do matter, Sagar," she said quietly. "To the people who truly see you, who love you, not for your pace, but your presence. And those who don't… they were never meant to journey with you."

A long silence stretched between them, thick with unspoken thoughts. The hum of the car was the only sound as Sagar stared at the road ahead, then at the empty curve where the Audi had vanished. When he finally spoke, his voice was low, almost as if he were piecing the truth together aloud.

"The Audi's Road wasn't mine, was it?"

Riddhi shook her head gently. "Nope."

He nodded slowly, as if acknowledging more than just the obvious.

"Their destination…" Sagar exhaled, voice low, almost thoughtful, "...was never meant to be mine."

"Different turn." Riddhi added softly, watching the road unfold ahead, "Different journey."

"I think we all do it," Riddhi said eventually. "We race people who aren't even in the same game. Promotions, relationships, vacations, kids, like there's a scoreboard no one agreed to but everyone's afraid of losing."

Sagar looked at her. "And by the time we realize…"

"The view's gone." Riddhi finished, her voice barely above a whisper, as she looked out the window at the rising sun.

The car rolled on.

They drove in silence.

But this time, it was the silence of realization.

This time, at a pace that honoured the road.

This time, they noticed the birds.

This time, they didn't miss the breeze.

Reflection

We live in a world obsessed with achievements. With fast promotions, fast lifestyles, and fast cars. And when someone zooms past us, a friend, a colleague, a stranger, we panic. Are we too slow? Are we missing out?

When we chase others, we abandon ourselves. And when we race toward destinations not meant for us, we miss the very beauty of the road ahead of us.

Chapter 2

The Speed Bias

"Judgment often accelerates faster than compassion, and crashes deeper."

The alarm buzzed.

7:30 a.m.

Sagar woke up with a smile. Sunday had been well spent with Riddhi; her mature, thoughtful perspective on life always left him feeling grounded. But as soon as he brushed away the sheets, reality crept in.

The day ahead needed planning. He had a meeting with the London client at 9:30 a.m., *again.* "The third presentation," he mumbled in irritation. *"What more do they want?"*

While making his bed and pulling open the curtains, Sagar mentally mapped his morning. He had to leave by 8:30 sharp; Monday morning traffic was always chaotic. Today, Riddhi was headed to Media House in Delhi, where the final design templates for the upcoming brand campaign were being reviewed.

After stepping out of the bathroom, he glanced at the clock.

8:05 a.m.

Okay, focus now.

He decided on his white shirt with dark blue trousers, a safe, crisp combination for what could be a big day. This presentation might finally close the deal. It could even swing his appraisal for the next year.

He opened his closet and looked for the white shirt.

But the shirt was missing.

He rummaged through all three racks of the wardrobe, nothing. A flicker of panic set in. The clock now read 8:15.

Then he remembered- the laundry. He had planned to iron the shirt on Sunday evening but hadn't returned home in time.

He dashed to the other room, and there the white short was smugly waiting on the ironing table.

Blowing out a frustrated breath, he plugged in the iron and began pressing the shirt even before the iron fully heated. The wrinkles refused to budge. He turned up the heat.

Still no luck.

Losing patience, he pressed the iron down firmly, and when he lifted it a few seconds later, a faint yellow scorch mark had bloomed.

8:20 a.m.

"Oh no… not today!"

He flung the shirt aside and dashed back to his closet, grabbing the first one he saw, a light blue shirt. It would work.

He tugged it on hastily. Just as he was buttoning it up, a button near the chest snapped off.

"You've got to be kidding me!" he growled.

Off came the light blue shirt, tossed angrily on the floor. He yanked out a brown one this time. "Brown with navy trousers, *lousy combo"*, he thought, "but at this point, aesthetics could go to hell."

Throwing on the shirt, socks, and shoes, he grabbed his laptop bag and jacket. His stomach rumbled. He hadn't even had coffee.

8:40 a.m.

No time for breakfast.

He slammed the door shut behind him and ran toward the lift. It was on the 23rd floor.

Seriously?

He waited, watching the numbers tick down... 22... 21....

And waited.

The lift stopped on every floor.

It was one of those mornings!!!

8:43 a.m.

The lift arrived, full to the brim. No one budged.

He caught the eye of a few acquaintances inside. They smiled. He didn't.

If he could, he'd have dragged someone out and stepped in. But instead, he bolted for the stairs, skipping two at a time.

The security guard stood to salute him. Sagar ignored it.

He sprinted toward his car.

Why is the parking lot so far?!

8:55 a.m.

He threw himself into the car, jammed the ignition button, and sped out of the complex like he was in a race.

The drive was reckless. Hard acceleration. Sudden braking. Angry honks. Loud curses.

Everyone seemed to be driving at a snail's pace.

Do people not have places to be? he fumed.

A small hatchback ambled in the fast lane. He tailgated aggressively until it moved aside. He cut off a bike at the next red light. At a U-turn, he barely missed scraping an old Maruti, shooting its elderly driver a withering look.

He reached the office, tires screeching slightly as he parked. It was 9:32 a.m.

He sprinted into the building, heart pounding, not from nerves, but from sheer rage and exertion.

Only when he sat in the meeting room did he realize he had forgotten the file that had the printouts of all the charts, which he had so diligently prepared, working all Saturday night.

No no no...

Since he had the soft copy of the charts, the presentation went on. He somehow managed the show. He had rehearsed it well enough, but his mind wasn't in it. The visuals were off. It was like watching a movie on mute; everything seemed to move, but nothing felt alive. His slides were there; the points he had prepared were there… but his presence wasn't. The moments he'd rehearsed with clarity felt muddled now, slightly offbeat, like a pianist missing every fourth note.

Conscious of the ill-matched outfit -Brown shirt, navy trousers- he imagined his colleagues gossiping about his sense of dressing. His thoughts distracted him through the slides, dulling his usual spark.

The meeting ended. Technically, it hadn't gone badly. But it hadn't landed either. The rhythm was broken. It was not his best work. And he knew it.

He left the room with a faint nod and a half-smile, unsure if he'd salvaged the opportunity or just delayed its collapse.

All afternoon, he dragged himself through work. People spoke. Emails pinged. But his mind stayed foggy, looping endlessly through the burnt shirt, the forgotten file, the mismatched outfit, the speed, the anger, the heat building inside him like a pressure cooker.

By evening, the tension had crusted over his skin like dried sweat. That's when he texted Riddhi.

"Coffee?"

"Usual place. 7:00?"

"See you."

That evening, over coffee at their usual café, Sagar met up with Riddhi and recounted his morning.

"The white shirt burned… the blue one lost a button… I ended up in this weird brown shirt–blue trousers combo. I forgot my file. And I drove like a maniac. Honestly, I was just one coffee short of losing my mind today," he said, shaking his head and laughing bitterly.

Riddhi smiled gently, "Sounds like Monday arrived with boxing gloves."

"Yeah, and it punched me square in the face," he muttered, stirring his coffee absentmindedly.

There was a pause.

Then, almost as an afterthought, he added, "You remember that black Scorpio from yesterday? The one that cut us off dangerously on the curve?"

Riddhi nodded, her expression cautious.

"I kept thinking about him today… especially when I found myself driving like a madman," Sagar said slowly.

"And somewhere between yelling at slow drivers and cursing traffic, it just hit me, what if *that Scorpio* was rushing for something important too?"

He leaned back, eyes narrowing in thought.

"What if his wife was in labour? Maybe his dad was in the hospital? Maybe he got some bad news. Maybe his kid was waiting for him and was alone. I don't know. But… what if he wasn't being arrogant? What if he was just overwhelmed?"

He paused, staring out the window. A boy was dragging a toy car across the café's outer bench, gently, almost lovingly. His mother sat beside him, scrolling through her phone. Ordinary, peaceful.

Riddhi didn't interrupt. She simply let him continue.

Sagar's voice softened, "It's strange, isn't it? How easy it is to believe that we're the only ones with a crisis. That *our* hurry is justified. That *we* deserve space on the road. But the moment someone else acts the same, we label them - reckless, arrogant, selfish."

Riddhi looked at him with quiet admiration. "That's a pretty big shift in perspective, Sagar."

He chuckled dryly. "Well, it took a burnt shirt, a broken button, a missing file, and a very grumpy breakfast-skipping version of me to get there."

She smiled. "Sometimes, the only way to slow down... is to be forced into chaos. That's when we see how fast we've been going, not just on the road, but in our heads."

He looked at her.

There it was again, her ability to name what he was only beginning to understand.

"I guess," he said after a while, "today wasn't about the shirt or the traffic or the file. It was about seeing how easily I can lose myself in a spiral… and how little grace I offer others when they're in their spiral."

Riddhi met his gaze. There was no need for a lecture. No moral lesson. Just presence.

And for the first time all day, Sagar felt his inner pace finally match the world around him.

The rush in his chest eased. The coffee stopped being lukewarm disappointment and became comfort. The noise of the café turned into a hum instead of a buzz.

Maybe this was the speed life needed.

Not the speed of urgency.

But the speed of understanding.

Reflection

We often see the world through our own windshield, shaped by our mood, our rush, our destination.

An unsmiling face feels cold. A speeding car feels reckless. A slow driver feels like an obstacle.

But rarely do we pause to consider - maybe the smile is missing because of pain, maybe the speed is for someone they're about to lose, maybe the slowness is caution born of past hurt.

Maybe the speed bias is real; we expect the world to move at our pace, in our way. We drive, judge, and move on, forgetting that others, too, are on their own roads, carrying their own storms.

Chapter 3

The Rearview Mirror

"The past is behind for a reason.
It is the road ahead that needs our eyes."

The alarm buzzed.

7:30 a.m.

The Tuesday morning sun crept lazily through the curtains, casting soft golden patterns on the wooden floor tiles in Sagar's bedroom. The winters were getting chillier with every passing day. There was a calm stillness to the day, a slowness that made him linger in bed for an extra minute. Today was Riddhi's turn to drive to the office, which meant he didn't have to rush. One less chore. One more luxury.

By 8:30 a.m., Sagar stepped out of his building just in time to see Riddhi's white sedan glide into the driveway, polished, composed, and elegant, just like the woman behind the wheel.

As he slid into the passenger seat, her fragrance enveloped him, familiar, soothing, like jasmine caught in a breeze.

"You look like a poetry book this morning," Sagar said, smiling as he admired her pastel cream cardigan, soft pink lip gloss that caught the sun just right, and a single rebellious strand of hair brushing against her cheek. The matching earrings peeked out from beneath her hair like little secrets.

"And you look like someone who hasn't ironed his shirt, and wore the jacket to cover the same," she quipped, raising an eyebrow with just the right amount of sass.

He laughed. "It's called effortless charm!"

Riddhi smilingly nodded and carefully steered the car out of the building. Sagar noticed that there was something about her today that felt a little heavier than usual, not unpleasant, just... deeper.

As they drove past the familiar turns, Sagar turned toward her.

"You okay?" he asked gently. "You're very quiet today. Thinking about something?

She didn't respond immediately.

The comfortable silence, the kind only two people who trust each other can share, lingered for a few moments.

Then, she took a slow breath and said, "Do you ever feel like some memories just refuse to fade, like they're etched in the rearview mirror? You keep looking forward, but they're always there, just behind you, following you, watching you."

Sagar didn't say anything. He turned toward her, truly listening.

She had her eyes fixed ahead on the road, and Sagar could see that she was pensive today.

Out of the windshield, Riddhi kept her eyes on the road and noticed the city waking up, vendors arranging their fruits in pyramid perfection, schoolchildren in uniforms marching towards their school buses, and the aroma of fresh parathas wafting from roadside eateries.

"My mom called this morning. Again," Riddhi began. "The same conversation, that I'm getting older, that it will be my 30th birthday next month, and I need to settle down, that once she's gone, I'll be left all alone."

She sighed. "I just don't get it. Why can't she accept that I don't want to get married? Why can't she see that I'm happy, just the way I am?"

Sagar stayed quiet. Listening.

Riddhi's voice grew softer. "Sagar, you know... both my parents were working in banks. Dad was a Branch Manager in a private bank, and Mom was an Assistant Manager in a state bank. They'd be back home by 5:30 every evening. But only one of them stepped into a second shift."

Her grip on the steering wheel tightened.

"Mom would walk in, crack a quick joke about the traffic, keep her dupatta aside, and head straight to the kitchen. And just like that, her 'second shift' would begin. Chopping onions, making dinner, washing dishes, and getting clothes sorted. Meanwhile, Dad would change into his kurta, call out to his walking group, and head out for his evening stroll. Of course, he took me along to give mom space, but it was never really about helping her."

She paused. The memory, though worn with time, still carried weight.

"You know, back then, there were no washing machines. Every Saturday, the back verandah would be lined with clothes - dozens of them, soaked in tubs of water. My school uniform, Dad's shirts, even Dadu's vests. She'd sit on a low stool, with a stick in one hand and detergent in the other, scrubbing and rinsing from morning till lunch. No fuss, no complaint. Just... doing it." She paused.

And then continued, "Every morning, cooking breakfast, packing dabbas, ironing clothes, helping Dadu with his meds. And somehow, she'd still leave for office at 9:15 sharp, looking like she hadn't lifted a finger."

Riddhi's eyes stayed on the road, but her voice held a smile now. A tired, fond smile.

"She was always cheerful, always joking, even with the maid, or the *sabziwala.* And at work, everyone respected her. She was honest, straight-talking, the one people turned to when things got messy. She had this effortless way of lifting people's spirits, even while carrying so much herself."

A silence settled in the car for a moment, heavy but warm.

"And when I offered to help, Mom would say, 'Beta, you study. I will manage." Her voice dropped. "She never complained. Not once."

"But then… her energy started to give up."

Riddhi's voice turned quiet, almost reverent. "She never said it aloud. Never complained. But I could see it. I could see the fatigue pooling in her eyes every evening, like shadows gathering behind a smile that still tried to stay bright."

She exhaled slowly, as if those memories still weighed fresh.

"She used to hum while kneading dough. But over the years, it faded. First into pauses... then into silence. The kind of silence that creeps in not because you're sad, but because you're just... spent."

Sagar swallowed, feeling her words settle somewhere in his chest, quiet and aching.

"She still smiled. Still served dinner with a joke. Still folded clothes with care. But the spark? It had dulled. Like a lamp that kept burning long after the oil had dried up. And none of us noticed, because she never let the light go out. She just dimmed herself to keep the rest of us glowing."

Riddhi blinked hard, her eyes on the road, her voice steady again.

"That's the thing about women like her, they're so good at managing everything, we forget to ask if they're okay. And they forget how to ask for help."

Sagar swallowed, feeling her words settle somewhere in his chest.

"But can I ever do that?" Her voice faltered for a moment, the question hanging in the air like something fragile and forbidden.

"Would I want to?" she continued, softer now. "To erase myself? To become invisible, bit by bit, so that others could shine brighter, live easier?"

She shook her head gently, as if answering not just Sagar, but herself.

"I've thought about it so many times. What if that's what love is supposed to look like? What if that's what being a woman means, shrinking, softening, stepping aside without being asked?"

She paused, her hands tightening on the steering wheel.

"I am ashamed to say this... but no. I can't. I won't. Not because I don't care, but because I've seen what that kind of caring costs. I've watched a woman I love, disappear inch by inch behind the curtains of duty and sacrifice. And I... I don't want that to be my story."

She glanced out the window, her voice steadier now.

"If love asks me to disappear, then maybe it isn't love at all. That's why I've made peace with being single," she continued. "I don't want to live a life where love means servitude. Where coming home means rolling out chapatis just because I'm the woman. Where being a mother means being the only parent expected to feed, soothe, and sacrifice. I want love and companionship, like equals, Sagar, but not at the cost of vanishing."

The car slowed as they approached a red light. She wiped a corner of her eye discreetly.

"I get it," Sagar said, gently. "I really do. My sister Madhu, do you remember, I told you about her divorce?"

He exhaled, watching the traffic crawl.

"She was brilliant in college. A university gold medallist in economics. Took up a core analytics role straight after her MBA. She loved her work, she still does. She had dreams of heading strategy for a global brand, not just for the title, but because her mind thrived on solving big problems. But the moment she got married, it was like the walls closed in."

Riddhi glanced at him, listening and thinking of Madhu Didi as she remembered her from that one Diwali gathering last year.

Draped in a soft cotton saree, her presence was serene, almost understated. There was a kindness in her smile, a warmth that put others at ease. But her eyes, gentle yet unwavering, held a quiet fire. The kind that didn't shout its ambition but carried it like a steady flame. She moved through the room with grace, but one could tell that this was a woman who knew exactly what she wanted and why it mattered.

Sagar continued, "Her in-laws didn't like her flying for conferences, saying 'a good wife doesn't stay overnight in hotels.' They expected her to quit within six months of her marriage. She couldn't even order food if she was tired, because, apparently, a good wife makes fresh chapatis every night. That was their idea of virtue."

A long silence followed.

"So, I know where you're coming from," he added. "I've seen what it does to a woman when her ambition is constantly made to feel like defiance."

Riddhi looked at him, despite herself, eyes curious. "How is Madhu Didi now?"

He grinned. "She's thriving. Re-married. To someone who makes her breakfast every morning. Packs her lunch. They fight about who gets to cook dinner. Their biggest debate last week was over paneer vs. tofu. That's the kind of marriage she has now."

Riddhi chuckled. "That's adorable!"

"Right?" Sagar nodded. "They laugh a lot. Their fridge has more sticky notes than magnets. And every one of those notes is love, in different fonts."

A beat of silence followed, not heavy, just full.

Then Sagar turned slightly in his seat. "You know, Riddhi… life's meant to be driven looking forward. We all have our rearview mirrors - some filled with pain, others with pride. But if we keep staring into them, we miss the road ahead."

She looked ahead, quietly.

"The rearview exists so we remember, not so we re-live. If the past were meant to guide us forever, the rearview mirror would be as big as the windshield. But it isn't. The windshield is wide and open, full of new turns, new landscapes, and new sunrises. It deserves our full gaze."

Riddhi nodded slowly. "That's beautiful."

"I have my moments," he grinned.

Then, with a playful grin and sudden lightness, he added casually, almost too casually, "Also, if you ever decide to marry me, I swear on my grandmother's recipe book, you will never have to cook a single meal. I'll handle it all. Breakfast in bed, candlelight dinners, rajma that will bring tears to your eyes... from joy, not spice. And if we have kids, I'll pack their lunchboxes with alphabet-shaped parathas and love notes. Your only job will be to show up and be your radiant self."

Riddhi gasped, a mix of disbelief and suppressed laughter. She stole a sideways glance at him, wide-eyed.

"Wait. Did you just propose to me?"

He smirked. "Could be. Or maybe it was just a passionate chef's pitch… with some emotional garnish."

She shook her head, her lips twitching as she fought back a full grin, cheeks tinged with a soft blush. And just like that, they both burst into giggles, letting the laughter fill the space, deliberately sidestepping the weight of what might have just been said.

The car rolled into the office parking. She turned off the ignition but didn't get out immediately.

"Thank you, Sagar. For listening. For not trying to fix it. Just… being there."

She wanted to ask if he meant it, the proposal, the dream, the promises wrapped in humour. But she held the question back. Some feelings needed to sit for a while, like a tea bag in warm water, to seep in its own time.

As they stepped out of the car, she shivered – was it the effect of Sagar's half-joke proposal, or was it the chill in the air? She was unsure. But they walked to the building side by side, not speaking, but the silence had shifted. It now held space, warmth, and an invitation, not to return to the past, but to step into something new on the road ahead.

A future that might just be waiting ahead, seen not in the rearview mirror, but through the windshield.

Reflection: A Glance, not a Gaze

The rearview mirror exists not to trap us, but to keep us aware. It reminds us of where we've come from, not to linger in regret, but to ensure we don't repeat what we've outgrown. We don't drive forward by staring backwards. And we don't build the future by replaying the past.

Some roles, expectations, and burdens belong to another time. They've passed, like the road behind.

So, let us just glance at the past, but not dwell over it. The road ahead is waiting, wide, open, and ours to define.

Chapter 4

Driving through the Fog

"Sometimes, it's not about chasing clarity,
it's about trusting it will find you, in its own time."

The alarm buzzed.

7:30 a.m.

Sagar peeked out from under his quilt. The chill in the air bit harder today. It was only Wednesday, the mid-week monotony weighed heavier when paired with cold mornings and restless minds.

He dragged himself out of bed and peered out of the window. But there was nothing to see, just a thick, unmoving curtain of fog that swallowed the world whole. From the ninth floor, even the outline of familiar trees and parked cars had vanished.

It was his turn to drive today. And visibility was near zero.

He sighed.

The world outside was still and silent. But inside, Sagar's heart and thoughts, it was anything but calm. The fog outside seemed to have crept into his mind, clouding his clarity, stirring the memory that refused to settle – his half-joke proposal to Riddhi the previous morning, and her being a little uptight throughout the day yesterday.

She hadn't brought it up. But then, neither had he.

Was it really a joke?

Had he gone too far?

Did he mean it?

What was she thinking about it? Laughing it off?

Or worse… was she offended?

With every glance they had shared yesterday playing on a loop in his mind, Sagar was trying to decipher the words that were never spoken.

He dressed in layers, not so much because of the cold, but because he felt emotionally exposed and unsure of himself. As he stepped out of his building and walked towards the parking lot, he zipped his jacket like one shields oneself before a storm.

By the time he stepped into the car, it was 8:25 a.m. Five minutes to pick up Riddhi. Right on time.

Switching the fog lights and hazard lights on, he pulled out of the parking lot.

Visibility was almost zero.

He switched on the heater and the fog lights. The windshield wipers moved in vain, brushing away what kept coming back- the stubborn curtain of thick fog. Even the headlights of oncoming vehicles appeared only at the last moment, as if the world was being sketched in real time, one frame at a time.

"Fog turns roads I've known for years into strangers," Sagar muttered. "Everything looks different."

Very guardedly, he eased out of the parking lot, inching forward with the caution of a man navigating memory, not just roads. In 500 meters, he reached.

A dark silhouette appeared in the distance. Her.

Riddhi stood in the fog wearing a charcoal overcoat, arms wrapped tightly around herself, her laptop bag slung over one shoulder like a reluctant accessory. She looked small, vulnerable, almost like the girl in a snow globe, caught in a flurry of thoughts and wind.

A minute later, Riddhi slipped into the passenger seat of Sagar's car, exhaling as the warm air inside wrapped around her like a soft blanket.

"God bless heated seats," she sighed, buckling up. "At this point, warmth feels like wealth."

"You and your dramatic metaphors," Sagar said, grinning. "Good morning! But I agree. Today it's brutal out there."

"I really hate driving in this kind of fog," Riddhi murmured, pulling her coat a little tighter. "My eyes start aching from all the squinting. Thank God, it is your turn to drive today."

Sagar gave a faint smile.

Truly, the fog was too dense today to navigate without straining the eyes.

The wipers swept across the glass in a steady rhythm but offered little to help visibility. Everything, inside his heart and outside the car, felt hazy.

Visibility couldn't have been more than ten meters. The road ahead was a grey sheet, unmarked, uncertain.

He was focusing hard. Too hard. Or maybe, too distracted by what was stirring within.

The image of Riddhi, not just in the seat beside him, but in his life, stirred something in Sagar. A strange mix of excitement and uncertainty fluttered within him, like a man standing at the edge of something beautiful, unsure whether taking a step closer would make it retreat... or open its arms to him.

He longed for what lay ahead, but wasn't just sure of how Riddhi might respond, he wasn't even certain if he was ready to stand by what he'd said, half in jest, the day before. And still, he couldn't summon the courage to seek clarity on what was quietly unfolding in his heart.

"God… this fog," Sagar murmured. "It's almost unreal, isn't it?"

He sighed and whispered almost to himself, "Strange how we keep inching forward, without actually knowing what lies just a few steps ahead of us."

Riddhi turned slightly to look at him. "You mean - while driving in the fog?"

His voice was even softer this time, almost distant. "Yeah. While driving in the fog. But also…. in life. It's like this, too. You follow the path, stay in your lane, try to keep moving – but you can't see what's coming. Not really."

Riddhi watched him more closely now. She could sense something beyond the spoken words.

"It seems you are thinking about something... more than what you are saying," she asked curiously. "Huh?"

He gave a short laugh, shaking his head and adjusting the defogger, more out of habit than hope. "Maybe I *am* talking about more than the road and life."

He turned slightly to look straight into Riddhi's eyes, nudging her to think of yesterday's proposal.

Riddhi skipped a heartbeat.

"And that is?" she said, hiding her nervousness. Outwardly, no expressions. Not a flinch.

Sagar sighed. "Lately, everything just feels…clouded. Not just the road ahead. Not just work. Not just decisions. Even the feelings I thought I had figured out... they're all…foggy."

Riddhi's expression softened. Her situation was no different.

Though she wasn't behind the wheel today, her eyes were strained too. Her heart, like the fog, was heavy and uncertain. Should she bring up yesterday's proposal? Was Sagar serious, or was it just a joke? No, this wasn't the right time. The road was treacherous, and Sagar needed to concentrate. But had he already forgotten about it? Or was he thinking about it too?

There was a moment of stillness between them, broken only by the hush of the tires against the damp road and the hypnotic swoosh of the wipers.

Frustrated and unclear, Sagar muttered, more to distract himself, "The office should declare work-from-home on a day like this. I can't even see the road divider, and I'm not sure which lane I'm in. The only thing I can follow are the taillights of the car ahead, and even those flicker into view only bit by bit."

Riddhi didn't answer immediately. Her gaze lingered on the fog-draped road ahead, where buildings, signboards, and even trees had vanished into a blank canvas.

A car overtook them. Not too fast, but slowly, deliberately, its taillights blinking briefly before fading into the fog ahead. It wasn't reckless. It wasn't hurried. It was almost graceful, like the driver knew exactly where they were going.

Sagar's eyes followed the car for a few seconds, then shifted back to the dimly visible road.

"Every time a car passes me on a foggy day like this, I can't help but wonder, how sure must the driver be? So confident, so clear about where they're headed. This feeling… feeling like everyone else has their path sorted and can see through this…. "

Gesturing to the fog outside, he continued, "…this fog… this noise… this uncertainty, while you're still staring through the haziness. Blank. Unsure."

Adding further, he said, "…and then I think… maybe they feel just as lost as I do. Maybe they're just better at hiding it. I don't know. But I always wonder… and somehow, I still marvel." Sagar said softly.

She wasn't sure either. But she could very well relate to Sagar.

"Maybe that's the thing, Sagar. We assume everyone else knows exactly what they're doing, while we're the only ones fumbling through. Maybe they, too, are as unsure as we are. But surely no one can really see too far ahead – not in *this* fog or in life."

"We all have our moments of uncertainty," she said softly.

"And in life," she continued, "most of the time, it's more like driving through this fog. You can't see more than a few steps ahead. You don't know if you're too slow or too late or on the wrong road entirely. And still, you keep going, because stopping isn't an option."

He nodded- eyes fixed on the glowing red taillights of the car ahead, the only thing visible in the white murk.

Sagar exhaled deeply, the defroster humming low. They were about 10 minutes away from the office now.

"Sector 48 Exit might be just around the corner," Sagar mumbled, more to himself than to Riddhi.

"I am not sure if we will be able to see the milestone at all in this fog today," he added apprehensively.

Riddhi turned to him, her voice steady. "But maybe that's the point. Maybe clarity isn't the starting line. Maybe it's the reward for choosing to move anyway. For not giving up when the road disappears. For taking the next turn even when you're terrified, it might be the wrong one."

"And that is exactly what I meant yesterday, Riddhi." Sagar quickly looked towards Riddhi, as she jumped at the mention of yesterday's discussion.

"You know," Sagar said finally, his eyes still fixed on the misty blur, "Taking the next turn, even if you are terrified that it is the wrong one, is the only way to go. Halting and not moving forward is not an option, even if your rearview mirror holds you back."

"I've been thinking and rethinking about what I said yesterday." He added with a resolve.

Riddhi turned to him, her breath briefly fogging the glass near her window.

"You mean the... proposal?" she asked, her tone teasing, though there was a softness to her voice that hadn't been there yesterday.

Sagar offered a sheepish smile. "Yeah. That. I mean... it started as a joke. But it wasn't, really. Somewhere between the rajma promises and alphabet parathas, I think I meant every word."

She didn't reply. She simply looked ahead, watching the fog swirl like the thoughts she hadn't allowed herself to fully entertain. The kind of thoughts that arrive uninvited and stay.

"I guess what I'm saying is," Sagar continued, "I know you're guarded. I know you have real, lived reasons to be. Society tries to squeeze women into roles they never asked for. I'm not trying to bulldoze my way into your life or rewrite your rules. I just want to say... if you ever choose to love, it should feel like companionship and freedom, not a duty roster."

The fog outside thickened.

And yet, something inside her began to clear.

She let out a small laugh, but it came with a sigh, that quiet, involuntary sound people make when something lands a little too close to the heart.

Just then, through the dense mist, the familiar blue board appeared like a sign from the universe:

Sector 48 Exit – 300 Metres Ahead

"There it is," Sagar said.

"Right on time," Riddhi whispered.

He took the turn with ease, merging onto the road that led to their office complex. They were almost there.

"I still can't see the whole road," he said quietly. "But I've stopped panicking about it. I've learned that even if you don't have a five-year plan, you just need to keep moving. The next ten metres will show up."

The car slowed as they neared the familiar office complex.

"Leap of faith," Sagar said quietly.

"What?"

"That's what makes the world go, isn't it? Not certainty. Just faith. That the road will appear. That we'll figure it out. That we'll find who we're meant to find, and what we're meant to do, even if it's only one hazy step at a time."

The car pulled into the parking space and settled into stillness.

Riddhi looked at him, her eyes softer now, and full of something unspoken. She didn't need to say yes. Not yet. But in that silence, something had shifted. The hesitation had thinned, just like the fog.

And with a small, almost shy smile, she said, "Maybe we've already found the way to our next ten metres ahead."

Sagar looked at her, really looked, and smiled back.

It wasn't clarity.

But it was something better.

It was the beginning of a shared road.

Reflection: Driving Through the Fog

Life doesn't hand us a map. It hands us a fogged-up windshield and a destination we can't quite see, only feel.

We long for sunny days for clarity. But unlike road trips on a bright day, life doesn't always come with certainty. It comes with foggy days, questions, doubts, and taillights to follow, one decision at a time.

And in those moments, when the way ahead is unclear and our hearts are unsure, we learn something precious:

Clarity isn't a prerequisite for movement. It's the outcome of faith. Faith that even if the road ahead is invisible, it still exists. Faith that when the moment is right, the way will show up. Faith that the right people, the ones who make the journey meaningful, may appear not with fireworks, but like a silhouette in the fog: quietly, unexpectedly, and just in time.

Because in the end, what matters most isn't seeing the whole route.

It's knowing eventually the road will show up, even if it's just ten metres at a time.

Chapter 5

The Blind Spot

"What we don't see still steers us."

The alarm buzzed.

7:30 a.m.

It was Thursday, and the sky was uncharacteristically clear for a Delhi morning in January. The sun peeked through soft clouds, as if deciding whether to rise fully or stay in contemplation a little longer.

Sagar stretched lazily, his heart still smiling from the shared glance that had lingered just a bit longer than usual when he had dropped Riddhi back a her place the previous evening. It hadn't been dramatic – just a moment of stillness, of eyes meeting, not saying much and yet saying a lot.

He got ready quickly. With fifteen minutes to spare, he whisked up his signature coffee, letting the soft hum of the electric whisk blend into his quiet joy. With a coffee mug in his hands, he stepped onto the balcony. The morning breeze was crisp but not harsh, and the birds were in conversation – chirping, fluttering, living. It felt like they were composing the music of his mood.

8:25 a.m.

Time to go.

He grabbed his laptop bag, still humming, and stepped out of the building just as Riddhi pulled up, punctual as always. Her hair was tied back today, and she wore a soft beige woollen stole wrapped casually around her.

"Dot on time!" she said. They exchanged a warm smile.

He chuckled, settling in and buckling up. "Miracles happen. But only when you drive."

They laughed, that comfortable laughter of people who've found a rhythm.

As she navigated out of the colony gate and onto the main road, she glanced sideways. "Did you manage to take Aunty to the doctor yesterday?"

Sagar nodded. "Yeah… finally. Her blood pressure's still on the higher side. But the doctor made some changes to her medication. Everything else is stable, thankfully."

Riddhi's expression softened. "She's lucky to have you. You're a good son."

"I can be good in many other roles," he winked, "in case you ever need to recruit?"

Riddhi rolled her eyes, playfully smacking his arm, "Sagarrrr, must you always turn everything into a joke?"

But inside, her heart betrayed her calm. It thudded a little too loudly, so for a fleeting second, she wondered if he could hear it too.

Sagar smiled and said solemnly, "Actually, yes. I'm serious about making up for all the times I've taken my mom for granted. Losing Dad when I was fourteen… it changed everything. Overnight, she had to become both the roof and the walls."

He looked out of the window, voice steady but edged with memory.

"She didn't fall apart. Not once. She just… stepped up. Took up a teaching job in the school nearby, paid the bills, managed the paperwork, kept my school running smoothly, and somehow still found time to ask if I'd eaten. There were nights I heard her crying in the kitchen. Not loud. Just the kind of cry that knows no one's listening. And yet the next morning, she'd be up early, ironing my uniform, packing my tiffin with extra aloo parathas like it was any other day."

Riddhi grew quiet, the weight of his words settling gently between them.

"She didn't have big dreams for herself," he added. "But she made sure I never had to shrink mine. That kind of strength… it doesn't shout. It endures."

Without a word, Riddhi reached over and gently touched his arm, and continued to drive with her usual calm, steady hands, light foot, eyes mindful of every movement. Sagar admired how her driving reflected her temperament: deliberate, present, unrushed.

They turned onto the main road just as the traffic began to thicken. A radio jingle faded into instrumental music, and the heater in the car hummed gently in the background.

That's when it happened.

A blaring horn.

A sudden flash of white.

A car zipped past from the left, cutting inches from Riddhi's front bumper.

She gasped, instinctively veering the wheel right and slamming the brake.

Sagar jolted in his seat, bracing against the dashboard.

"Whoa," he breathed, looking behind. "Where did that come from?"

Riddhi exhaled slowly, her knuckles still white on the wheel.

"I didn't see him," she said, catching her breath. "He was in my blind spot."

They sat in silence for a moment. Not from fear, but from recognition.

The hum of the engine filled the space between their words as she regained control and merged carefully back into the lane.

A few seconds passed.

Then Sagar spoke, his voice gentler now, curious. "That's the thing about blind spots, isn't it? You don't even know something's coming until it's already arrived."

Riddhi glanced at him, thoughtful. "I checked my mirror. I checked the road," she murmured. "But he wasn't in either. And then he just… appeared. Out of nowhere."

"No wonder the Blind Spot Indicators in the newer models of cars are such a critical safety feature," Sagar said quietly. "One tiny blink can be the difference between calm and chaos."

"All it does is signal, there's something here you can't see. That one flash can often be the difference between safety and collision," he added, his gaze distant, caught somewhere between memory and meaning.

Riddhi looked ahead, the traffic weaving like thought trails. "Sometimes, I think life has a way of honking loud enough to jolt us. Like that guy just did. Just enough to make us notice something we've been blind to."

Sagar leaned back, his mind shifting gears from the road to something deeper.

"What if we had those indicators in real life, too?" he said. "For conversations. For relationships. For ourselves."

He continued, his expression turning thoughtful.

"Wouldn't it be amazing," he continued slowly, "if we had something like - an emotional or behavioural blind spot indicator?"

Riddhi glanced at him, intrigued.

"You know," he continued, "some indicator that blinked gently every time we were about to say something hurtful without knowing. Or when we dismissed someone else's idea, thinking we were helping. Or… when we failed to notice someone withdrawing from us quietly."

Riddhi smiled softly. "That's what self-awareness is meant to be, right? That inner signal. But it takes years to develop, and even then, it flickers sometimes."

"Reminds me of something we learnt back in psych class," Sagar said, warming up to the thought. "The Johari Window. Four quadrants, what we know about ourselves and what others know about us."

"Oh yeah," Riddhi said, remembering. "Known to self, known to others… unknown to self, unknown to others."

He nodded. "And in there is that infamous third quadrant, the blind spot, also called the bad breath zone. What others see and observe about us, but we don't."

"And unless someone points it out with love," Riddhi added, "we stay blind. Keep repeating the same patterns. Maybe smelling bad or hurting others without meaning to."

"Which makes those people, who gently show us our blind spots, kind of like human blind spot indicators. They don't just reflect us, they protect us." Sagar said with a smile.

They drove a while in silence, each digesting the metaphor. Lived.

Sagar's gaze followed a cyclist gliding along the edge of the road. He wasn't sure why, but some flashes from the previous day's meeting in the office started to run in front of his eyes. One hand rested on the windowsill, fingers tapping without rhythm.

After a long silence, he spoke.

"Can I ask you something?"

"Always," Riddhi replied, her tone open.

He hesitated.

"Do you think I… dominate meetings?"

She glanced at him, then back to the road. "Why do you ask?"

Sagar started recounting the events from the previous day's meeting.

"Tanya," Sagar said, almost thoughtfully. "She's the junior strategist in my team. Quiet, mostly. But not unsure. You can tell she listens more than she speaks, and when she does speak, it's usually worth hearing. Yesterday, she raised a point, a new angle for the new campaign. It was fresh. Considered. As she shared her idea, her voice trembled a little, but there was clarity behind it. Conviction."

He paused, watching the rows of traffic inch forward.

"She doesn't push her way into conversations. She waits for space to speak. And yesterday, when she was presenting her idea … before she could finish, I think I jumped in."

"I thought I was helping. I tweaked her idea mid-sentence. Reworded it. Sharpened it. Made it more… pitch-worthy, or so I believed" He paused before continuing, "But she went silent after that."

Riddhi didn't speak, just listened, the way good mirrors do.

Sagar continued, "At the time, I felt like I was improving it. Like I was showing support. But later… when I looked at her across the table, there was something different in her eyes. Hesitation? Discomfort? Disengagement, maybe."

He shook his head slightly, as though trying to dust something off his conscience.

"And then it struck me… I didn't just tweak her idea. I took over her space. Her moment. Maybe I was just polishing it with my voice because I thought it sounded better coming from me. And in doing that… I erased her. Not the idea, but her."

Riddhi's gaze remained on the road, but her awareness had turned fully to him.

He added quietly, "And that's not all. There were other times, in the same meeting. When Rohan was speaking, measured as always, choosing his words like he's laying down bricks, one piece at a time, I redirected the point. He didn't push back, just gave a small nod and let it go. That's how he is. Calm. Thoughtful. A little too polite for rooms that reward volume and pitch."

He exhaled and leaned his elbow against the door, resting his head in his hand.

"But when Ankit did the same to me, cutting me mid-sentence to insert his viewpoint, that irritated me. And Ankit's not even rude, he's just… assertive. Sharp-edged. Always ready to take space, even if he has to carve it. But in that moment, it felt like my rhythm had been tripped. Like, I didn't matter as much."

There was a beat of silence, filled only by the ticking of the indicator light as they waited at a red signal.

Sagar turned slowly toward Riddhi, his voice now softer. "What if I've been doing that to others for a long time and just didn't know? Cutting their rhythm? What if I've kept other people, their contributions, in the blind spot of my success story? What if my presence in a room dims someone else's courage to speak, just like it did to mine when Ankit asserted his point yesterday?"

Riddhi finally looked at him. Not with judgment. But with care. The kind that lets someone unfold without fear of being unloved.

She placed her hand briefly on his wrist. "That awareness right there, Sagar, that's your blind spot indicator blinking. It's not about being perfect. It's about noticing when your indicator blinks and having the humility to take cognizance of the same."

He gave a faint nod, as if receiving something more important than advice, grace.

"I've always prided myself on being articulate. Present. Quick to contribute. But maybe… maybe I've confused dominance with value."

Riddhi smiled gently. "We all do that, especially when we've been rewarded for it. You're a natural leader. People listen to you. But sometimes, the best leaders know when to hold silence, and let others arrive at their own voice."

The car began to move again. The city outside blurred in and out of focus, like thoughts settling into place.

"Blind spots aren't weaknesses," Riddhi added. "They're parts of us; we haven't turned towards yet. And it takes courage to do that. Most people spend years avoiding them."

Sagar sat quietly, the weight of the conversation anchoring him in a deeper space within himself. A part of him wanted to rewind all those moments and offer them back to the people he had spoken over. But he knew real change wasn't in apology alone, it was in awareness moving forward.

As they neared the office, he said softly, "Thanks, Riddhi. For not blinking away from this conversation."

She smiled, slowing the car to enter the office gate. "We all need someone to be our blind spot indicators sometimes."

He smiled back, the kind of smile that rises not from comfort, but from clarity.

And as they parked and stepped out into the day ahead, the sun had risen fully now, lighting not just the path ahead, but corners of the self that had stayed in the shade too long.

And something about today's drive lingered with them, not the shock, not the driver, but the phrase:

"Blind spot."

It stayed with them like a whisper echoing at the edge of a thought.

Reflection: Things We Don't Know We Carry

Blind spots aren't signs of weakness. They're signs of being human. Reminders that we are layered. Complex. In progress.

Seeing our blind spots isn't about shame. It's about growth. About learning to receive feedback not as an attack, but as guidance.

And to honour the people who hold up the mirror with love, not judgement.

Because what we don't see… still shapes us. And the moment we *do* see it, we gain a new direction and a wider view of the road ahead.

Chapter 6

Traffic Light

"Sometimes, it's not the world that needs changing, just the way we see it."

It was Friday. The thin veil of mist still clung to the streets, but the city was slowly warming up to the day. Sagar was at the wheel today, and Riddhi sat beside him, hair tied in a loose bun, fiddling with the playlist to find the music to go with the mood for today. She settled for Satinder Sartaaj's *Rutba* and checked with Sagar if he was good with her choice. Sagar gave her a thumbs-up.

As they neared the large intersection near Cyber Park, Sagar saw the traffic light ahead turning amber. Then green… blinking once… twice…

3…2…1…Red.

They stopped. The digital timer lit up in bold red:

120…119…118…

Theirs was the first car in line. Just behind them, a grey EcoSport pulled up, and then more vehicles followed and kept joining the wait. Buses... autorickshaws... motorcycles... big cars… small cars…waiting patiently.

The world slowed.

For a moment, it was just silence. Broken occasionally by the hustle, each time the traffic light turned green for some lane.

Riddhi, leaning back, said softly, “You know, traffic lights are oddly reassuring. They don’t judge. They just ask you to pause… no matter who you are.”

Sagar smiled, nodding. “And no matter how late you are.”

They chuckled.

And then, HOOOOONK.

A loud, sharp blast pierced their moment.

Sagar glanced in the rearview mirror, unsure if it was meant for him.

Another burst – honk, honk.

Behind them, the grey EcoSport was honking incessantly, the driver inside motioning animatedly. The honking continued, rhythmic, insistent.

Sagar looked at the timer.

97 seconds to go.

He frowned. “What’s wrong with this guy? Can't he see the red light? Some people are just... so impatient.”

The honking didn’t stop.

Now irritated, Sagar raised his hand, gesturing behind to the driver of the EcoSport, through the rearview mirror. A calm but clearly annoyed wave, asking, “Why? Look at the light, buddy!”

The honking didn’t stop.

A slow wave of irritation rolled over him. He could feel it in his neck, tightening, rising into his jaw. The kind of slow-burning annoyance that blinds you to logic. That narrows your vision into judgment.

He declared, "Unbelievable! People have zero patience."

Sagar stared ahead, the red light still glowing, the timer now at 74 seconds.

Sagar gestured again in the rearview mirror, exasperated, as if to say, *"What do you expect me to do? Fly over the red light like an airplane?"*

But the driver behind didn't back down. He raised both hands, animatedly pointing downward, then waving with increasing urgency. His movements were frantic, trying to communicate something beyond the irritation Sagar had assumed.

Sagar squinted, trying to decode the gestures.

And then, like a jolt of lightning, it hit him.

Sagar's car was rolling backwards.

It happened in a blink. The car rolled back, just a little more, just enough to send a shiver of realization through him.

Sagar's foot was resting lightly on the brake, but not enough to hold the car fully, and the handbrake was not on. The slope was mild, but real.

And the EcoSport behind was just inches away. The man was honking not out of impatience, but warning of the impending crash, alerting Sagar to apply the brakes immediately.

His honks were warning, not noise.

Realisation dawned on Sagar. Quietly, almost sheepishly, he pulled the handbrake.

Sagar sank back in his seat, the red hue of the traffic light spilling across his face like quiet shame. "And I thought he was the idiot."

He looked into the rearview mirror again, this time, not with irritation, but with gratitude. The man behind wasn't even looking anymore. Crisis averted. No thanks asked, none given.

"We're so quick to judge, aren't we? Sagar added. "I was so sure he was wrong. Turns out, he was the one looking out for us."

Riddhi looked at him, eyes soft with understanding.

The moment hung in the air, heavy and thoughtful.

The kind of moment that made you reflect not just on the traffic, but on life.

As the light turned green and their car moved forward with the flow of traffic, a comfortable silence followed.

Riddhi stayed silent for a moment, then spoke softly. "You know… your little brake moment back there reminded me of something I'm not too proud of."

Sagar looked at her, interested.

"There's this guy at work, Varun. Works in analytics. Not the most expressive person. Quiet, always keeps to himself. We were working on this quarterly review presentation together. I needed data from his side to build my slides, and I had told him quite clearly that I needed it by Monday morning. But Monday came and went, nothing."

She shifted slightly in her seat, eyes on the road. "I was livid. This was going to the CEO, and every passing moment was crucial."

She paused. "So, I called him in, ready to give him a piece of my mind. And just as I began, he looked at me with these wide, nervous eyes and said, *'Ma'am, I sent it on Sunday night. I worked the entire weekend to put it together, as I realized how important it was for you. I was even worried you hadn't replied.'*"

Sagar raised an eyebrow. "So, where was it?"

Riddhi smiled. "In a shared folder. He had followed the protocol we always used. I just... forgot. I was so caught up; I expected it to be in my inbox. And I almost humiliated someone for *my* oversight."

Sagar let out a soft whistle.

"I felt like the worst human being," she said, her voice quieter now. "I thought I was being professional, demanding accountability. But I had built a whole story in my head of someone being irresponsible, disrespectful, lazy, when the reality was something else entirely."

She sighed, brushing a strand of hair behind her ear. "That incident taught me something important."

Riddhi paused, then added with a faint, thoughtful smile, "You know, ever since that day… I've changed the way I ask people things."

Sagar looked at her, curious.

She continued, "Earlier, I'd say things like, *'Why haven't you sent me the report?'* or *'I told you I needed it today'* – straight, pointed, confrontational. It felt natural. Efficient. Clear.

But after what happened with Varun, I am very mindful of my words."

She glanced at Sagar. "Now, instead of assuming someone hasn't done what I asked for, I simply say, *'Hey, I don't seem to find it in my inbox. Could you please resend?'* It leaves room for grace. For the possibility that it was sent, and I missed it. Or that they were trying to send it, but something came in the way. Or even that they forgot – it doesn't put them on the defence."

Sagar smiled slowly, "That's not just kindness. That's wisdom. Growth. Maturity."

Riddhi smiled. Murmured, "Nothing of the sort! It is just that it is incredible how much relationships – at work, at home – are shaped not by what we say, but by how we say it. That one sentence shift can save so many conversations from turning sour. It offers the other person dignity, even if they've slipped up."

"And, many a times, dignity is all someone needs to stay accountable," Sagar added.

"Ironic, isn't it? The more secure we are in ourselves, the less we need to assert control over others. The softer our tone, the deeper our impact." Riddhi murmured.

Sagar glanced sideways. "You know," he said quietly, "every time you say something that makes me think a little deeper… I fall a little further."

Riddhi turned towards him, her eyes searching his face, half surprised, half unsure if she'd heard right.

He didn't look at her. Just kept his eyes on the road, as if the confession was too fragile to meet her gaze.

She smiled, her voice barely a whisper, "And here I was thinking you only fall for jokes and jalebis."

Sagar grinned, still not turning. "Well… some days I crave sweetness. Other days, depth. And with you... I get both."

Riddhi's cheeks flushed, and for the first time in a long while, she didn't know what to say.

But maybe she didn't need to.

Reflection – When Vision Shifts

The world softens the moment we shift from "Why did they do this to me?" to "What might they be going through?"

It takes courage to open the window of our view wider- to let another's truth enter, to admit we may have been wrong, and in that opening… perspective blooms. Judgment melts into understanding. Assumption bows to empathy.

Not from where I stand.

Not from where you stand.

But from the quiet space in between,

Where our perspectives meet,

And become one.

Chapter 7

You have arrived!

"In life's journey, purpose is the truest destination."

The alarm buzzed.

4:00 a.m.

For a moment, Sagar blinked into the darkness, disoriented, caught somewhere between dream and waking. But then, like a switch flipping, he remembered.

Chakrata.

The long weekend.

Just the two of them.

A soft flutter stirred in his chest. A quiet anticipation. The kind that hums beneath the surface when you're on the cusp of something real. He had packed his bag the night before - sweaters, camera-and had set the car keys right by the door.

By 4:45 a.m., he was outside Riddhi's apartment, headlights casting golden beams through the sleepy stillness. The city hadn't quite woken up yet. The streets were hushed, wearing a blanket of dew and silence.

Riddhi stepped out, wrapped in a soft stole, her hair in a low ponytail, and a travel mug in hand.

"Coffee?" she offered with a smile, sliding into the passenger seat.

"Lifesaver," Sagar grinned, taking a sip. "You're my favourite, did I tell you?"

"Flattery before sunrise, ambitious!" she teased.

By 5:00 a.m., their car was gliding onto the open highway, like a bird on a long flight, wings stretched, free from the clamour of deadlines and calendar invites.

Streetlights gave way to morning mist. The amber glow of the city slowly receded behind them as fields, silhouettes of trees, and distant hills began to take shape ahead. The sky was still indigo, but the promise of dawn sat quietly on the horizon.

Sagar tapped a few buttons on the screen and set the coordinates for their resort in Chakrata.

7 hours 15 minutes. 346 Kms displayed Google Maps and announced –

"Keep going straight for 46 kms. You are on the fastest route. You will reach your destination by 12:15 p.m."

He muted the GPS.

Fiddling with the playlist, he selected *Instrumental Retro Bollywood Classics,* a soft stream of nostalgia that filled the car like warm sunlight.

Leaning back into his seat, he set the cruise control to 70 km/hr, allowing the road to take over. The car hummed gently, a quiet companion in motion.

Beside him, Riddhi sat quietly, sipping her coffee. Her eyes watched the road, but her mind was clearly elsewhere.

Sagar glanced sideways.

"Sleepy? Huh?" he nudged.

She shook her head, smiling faintly. "No. Not at all. I am at my best in these wee morning hours. I was just thinking and… honestly, kind of in awe."

He raised an eyebrow. "Of?"

She gestured to the screen. "That voice. That line. *'You will reach your destination by 12:15.'* Just like that. So confident. It knows exactly which path to take, where we need to turn, and when we'll arrive. No confusion. No second-guessing. It's amazing."

She paused, then added, "Isn't it funny that we never question the GPS? We just… follow it. No drama. No panic."

Sagar chuckled softly. "You sound like you're talking about more than just our drive on the highway."

Riddhi let out a short laugh and turned slightly toward him. Her voice softened. "Maybe I am."

There was a silence, comfortable but charged with thought.

"Wouldn't it be something," she continued, "if life came with GPS? You know… guiding us to the right job, right decision, right partner."

"You are right…. But the GPS guides you only when you *know* where you want to go, i.e. the coordinates for your desired destination. Without it, you just keep moving, with the visible network of roads, but no indication of the road that you should take. Beautiful views, yes, but no arrival.

You might reach somewhere, but not necessarily where you were meant to be." Sagar reflected.

Riddhi looked out the window, the rising sun catching the edges of her profile.

"Hmmm…. Right…. Without it, any road would do," she whispered. "And we'd mistake motion for meaning."

The car moved through the silence that followed, as if giving space for the weight of her words to settle.

"Speed is seductive," Sagar said after a while. "You feel alive, in control. But direction, that's where the truth lies."

Riddhi nodded. "It's not about how fast we're going. It's about *where* we're going. And *why*?"

Riddhi shifted slightly, folding her arms as the warmth of sunlight began to lace the sky with golden threads.

"Have you ever wondered," she asked quietly, "what your loved ones will say about you when you're gone. Like forever. Dead?"

Sagar turned to her. The question lingered like mist, gentle, but impossible to ignore.

"I mean," she continued, "really say. Not just the goodbyes or the rituals, but the stories they'll remember when they sit together after everything. The things they'll tell about you… or whisper to themselves when they miss you."

Adding contemplatively, she continued, "Would I want them to say things like- That Riddhi had a sea-facing apartment? That she wore a luxury brand? Or would I rather have someone say, she listened without interrupting… she showed up when it mattered… she gave more than she took."

Sagar kept his eyes on the road, but his silence deepened, no longer from distraction, but from the weight of the question Riddhi had just offered.

He exhaled slowly, as if releasing years of noise.

"You know," he said quietly, "sometimes I wonder if we've been taught to measure life with the wrong ruler."

Riddhi looked at him.

He continued, "We count possessions… promotions… the square footage of our homes, the digits in our salaries. Our bank balance. Followers on LinkedIn or Instagram. Friends on Facebook."

"But no one ever talks about measuring soulprint. Not footprint, *soulprint.* The quiet ways we leave people feeling seen."

He glanced sideways at her, his voice steady, reflective as he continued, "You asked what people will say after we're gone… I think about that a lot. And I hope… I really hope they don't just say I was driven or accomplished or that I worked hard. I hope they say I made people *feel* safe. *Feel* cared for. That I protected moments, not just targets."

"I know there are moments when I forget all about my *soulprint* and am driven only by performance and achievements, but then, there are times - gentle nudges, to remind me of my destination and re-route me to the right destination. Reminder that I want to be remembered as the kind of person you'd want next to you, not because I had answers, but because I'd stay even when there weren't any. That I lifted people when they were feeling low."

He paused, letting the trees and winding hills pass them by in silence.

"And maybe that's the real wealth we leave behind," Riddhi continued, softer now. "Not what we built with our ambition, but what we built with our attention. Not the brands we wore, but the burdens we lightened. Maybe at the end, no one remembers our LinkedIn summary. They remember how we made them feel when they were breaking."

The car gently curved along a hairpin bend, as though even the road was listening.

"And if that's what we want to be remembered for," Sagar added, "maybe that's what we need to start living for. That is what our life's GPS coordinates ought to be."

Silence.

And then he continued after a pause, "One ambition to the next. We forget that *those memories*, the ones that stay behind, aren't built by what we earned. They're built by *how* we lived. Our purpose on this earth."

Riddhi looked out at the road unspooling endlessly ahead.

A breeze fluttered through the slightly open window. The music played on, slow, reflective, like an old song you didn't know you remembered.

Riddhi softly brought up her thoughts, "Our purpose. Our calling. It's like that book I once read, *The Five People You Meet in Heaven* by Mitch Albom. Ever read it?"

"Nah. What is it about?"

"The protagonist, Eddie," she said, "thought his life didn't matter. He was just a maintenance guy in an amusement park. Every day, fixing rides. Oiling bolts. Just… routine."

She paused. "But when he died, he found out that all those ordinary days of his days on earth had actually saved lives. Children who didn't fall off malfunctioning rides. Families that got to laugh together because he kept everything running, quietly, in the background. He never got applause. But he gave his life to something meaningful. Even if it didn't look 'special' from the outside."

Sagar didn't speak, but his stillness said he was listening with more than just his ears.

Riddhi added, her voice soft but steady, "That book changed me, Sagar. It made me stop chasing after some grand, dramatic idea of purpose, as if it were a mountain I had to climb, or a spotlight waiting for me to stand in. For the longest time, I thought that my *purpose on this earth or my calling* had to look like something extraordinary. Like changing the world. Being known. Doing something that people would write about."

She looked out of the window, watching the fields blur into golden streaks in the morning light. Her tone grew more contemplative.

"But reading that book… it shook something in me. Eddie wasn't famous. He didn't build an empire. He fixed bolts and oiled gears. He stayed behind the scenes so others could feel joy and be safe. And not once did he think his life meant anything. But when it was all over, he was shown that those small, silent acts made all the difference. Made the world a better place."

Sagar glanced at her, eyebrows furrowed slightly, not out of confusion, but realization.

Riddhi continued, "It made me wonder… what if our purpose isn't a destination at all? What if it's how we move through each day? How we show up for others, even when no one is watching. The integrity in our work. The grace in how we speak. The effort we make to listen, to really listen. What if purpose is not some distant calling, but the way we carry ordinary moments?"

There was a pause.

Sagar nodded slowly. "You're saying... what if we're already living our purpose, but we're too busy looking for something flashier, something louder, to notice?"

"Exactly," Riddhi said. "And maybe that's why so many of us feel lost. Because we're trying to find something *out there*... when it's been *right here* all along. In our classrooms. In our roles as teachers. In our homes. In our workplace. Our hospitals. Our desks. Our words. Our colleagues. Our family members. Our help. Our community."

She turned back to him, eyes sincere. "I think the mistake we make is waiting for life to give us clarity before we give it meaning. But maybe it's the other way around. Maybe clarity *comes* when we give ourselves fully to what's already in front of us."

Just then, they both observed a flicker on the GPS screen. It read,

"Rerouting. You are still on the fastest route. You will reach your destination by 12:20 p.m."

Sagar blinked, then chuckled softly. "Ah, I must've missed that left turn."

He glanced at Riddhi. "See? No yelling. No scolding. Just... *Rerouting*."

He paused, hands lightly resting on the steering wheel, as if letting the metaphor land before continuing.

"And isn't this fascinating?" he said, his voice warm with wonder. "Even when you go wrong, go astray, miss an exit or take a wrong lane, GPS simply, *calmly*, reroutes. No, 'I told you so.' No drama. No shame. Just a quiet, persistent nudge back on track."

He exhaled, eyes still on the road but mind somewhere deeper.

"How beautiful it would be," Sagar mused, "if life worked the same way. If *we* worked the same way. If, when, someone messed up, missed a step, made a poor decision, lost their way, we didn't attack them, didn't rush to blame. We just… gently helped them reroute."

He turned to Riddhi, softer now. "Imagine if we offered that same grace to ourselves. No harsh self-talk. No spiralling guilt. Just a calm inner voice saying, *'It's okay. Let's find another way. We're still going to get there.'*"

The silence between them felt full, not empty. The kind that invites reflection, not discomfort.

Sagar continued, "I think that's one of the most powerful gifts we can give each other. Not just direction, but *compassionate understanding*. The kind that doesn't make you feel smaller for needing it."

He tapped the dashboard lightly, as if saluting the GPS.

"It's like the universe saying, *'I still believe in your destination, even if you took a detour.'*"

Riddhi smiled, quietly moved.

Reflective silence. Eyes still on the long, winding road ahead.

The GPS chimed softly again:

"Continue straight for 107 kilometres."

The car moved forward steadily and quietly. The mountains grew closer, inviting and vast. They carried no billboards, no accolades, just presence.

Reflection: Soulprint

We spend life chasing destinations - titles, milestones, maps with pins - as if arrival is out there, somewhere ahead.

But maybe the calling of our life isn't out there waiting to be found, but right here, waiting to be lived? Not in the angle of our incline, but in the stillness of how we show up for others. Because in the end, no one remembers how fast we drove. They remember how deeply we cared.

Maybe that's when we truly arrive, not at the destination, but in who we become on the way, and that is when our soul's GPS whispers -

You have arrived!

Chapter 8

Hand brake

"Not every journey need speed, some just need a release of resistance."

The winding mountain road curled like a serpent through the hills; its edges laced with pine trees and mist. The sky above them was a soft shade of grey, carrying the scent of rain that had passed not long ago. Wet leaves shimmered on the road, and every curve demanded the driver's full presence.

Yesterday had been dreamlike.

They had reached Chakrata by late afternoon, checked into their modest hilltop hotel, and after a quick freshen-up, wandered into the dense embrace of the forest trails. The earth smelled of pine needles and moss. They had walked in silence for long stretches, it was the kind of surreal beauty that makes you forget emails, clocks, and headlines. That evening ended with steaming momos from a local shack and the plan to visit the highest peak in Chakrata the next morning: Chilmiri Neck.

Chilmiri Top, as the locals affectionately called it, lay about three kilometres from the main market area. But in mountain terms, three kilometres could stretch like eternity, especially when the path is steep, narrow, and laced with sharp bends and sheer drops. It wasn't just a drive; it was a commitment.

And in the early morning hours today, the little drizzle had added to the beauty of the place, making the trees greener and roads blacker…and also riskier and dangerous. Sagar was at the wheel, eyes alert but calm, guiding the car through the steepest ascent they had faced so far. Riddhi sat beside him, her window slightly rolled down, hair dancing gently in the breeze, her mind somewhere between the clouds outside and the memories within.

Riddhi's phone rang.

It was Sarita, her oldest friend, the keeper of childhood secrets and college giggles, the first one to read her poems and the last one to leave any party they hosted together.

"Hi Sariii!" Riddhi beamed, instinctively softening her voice. "You, okay?"

The chat began lightly, with the usual back-and-forth, how Sarita's three-year-old daughter, Raya, was doing and all the tantrums she was throwing. How her husband, Vikram, a corporate big-shot, was away most of the time on business trips, and how the paint-by-numbers mountain landscape she had sworn she'd finish last year was still lying incomplete. But gradually, Riddhi's tone changed. Her voice grew slower, her questions more measured.

Sagar could sense the undercurrent of worry beginning to surface.

When the call ended, Riddhi held her phone a little longer than usual, as if still holding Sarita's hand through it.

Sagar didn't pry, but his concern sat plainly in his voice. "Everything okay with Sarita?"

Riddhi sighed, looking straight ahead. "She's struggling."

She paused, then continued, "You know how brilliant she's always been. The topper, the award-winning orator, the star employee. During pregnancy, she took a break, a mutual decision with Vikram. But now, it's been three years. She's been applying for jobs for the last six months, but nothing's worked out yet. And she's not just feeling rejected professionally... she's doubting herself on every front. Says she doesn't even feel like a good mother some days. She's begun to associate the pause in her career with Raya's birth, and it's eating her from inside."

Sagar didn't speak immediately. The car climbed slowly around another curve. The incline steepened, and he shifted gears with practised ease. The engine grumbled but obeyed.

He let the silence stretch, not out of discomfort but reverence, like a moment of silence at a sacred place. Then, at a particularly steep bend, he slowed the car and paused.

The road narrowed here. One wrong move, and the drop would be unforgiving. He pulled the handbrake gently and kept his foot ready on the clutch.

"You know," he said, eyes still on the road ahead, "in an uphill drive," he began, "the balance between the handbrake and acceleration is everything."

Riddhi turned toward him, curious.

"It's one of the hardest things to master, especially for new drivers." He continued. "If you keep pressing the accelerator but don't release the handbrake, the car struggles, overheats... eventually burns out. And if you release the brake too soon and don't accelerate enough, you roll back. Both are dangerous. Both lead to panic."

Riddhi nodded, already beginning to see the dots he was connecting.

"Sarita seems to be wanting to accelerate now," he said gently. "Applying for jobs, prepping for interviews, updating her resume. But mentally... emotionally... her handbrake is still on. That voice in her head telling her she's not good enough anymore, that's the handbrake."

Riddhi nodded slowly, eyes fixed on the road ahead.

"She's trying to climb uphill with the handbrake pulled tight," she said. "And it's not just the struggle, it's how she's begun to see herself in that struggle. Like she's no longer capable. Like she's failed at something permanent."

Sagar tapped the steering wheel gently, thoughtfully. "You know what that reminds me of? Carol Dweck's research on- 'Mindset'. The idea that some of us carry a fixed mindset, believing that our abilities, intelligence, and worth are static. Unchangeable. So, if we fail once or face rejection, we take it as a statement of identity: *I'm not good enough.*"

Riddhi turned toward him, interested. "And the opposite is a growth mindset, right? Where challenges aren't judgments, they're invitations. To evolve. To adapt."

"Exactly," Sagar said, glancing briefly at her. "Sarita is brilliant. But somewhere along the way, life convinced her that if she's not constantly winning, she's no longer worthy. That her career break was a derailment, not a redirection. That a pause in achievement equals a pause in value."

Riddhi looked out at the trees flickering past like memories. "And the worst part is... she probably doesn't even realize she's stuck in a fixed mindset. It wears a very clever disguise- it sounds like humility, or realism, or responsibility. But underneath, it's fear of change. Fear of failure. Fear of being seen as… as less."

They rounded a steep curve, the tires hugging the road with care.

Sagar added, "A growth mindset doesn't guarantee success. But it guarantees motion. It says, *I may not be there yet, but I'm not defined by where I am.*"

Riddhi smiled faintly. "Like taking your foot off the brake, not to speed up blindly, but to *allow* the movement. To believe that maybe... the car can handle the climb."

There was a silence. The kind that didn't feel empty, but full of unsaid understanding.

"And it's not just Sarita," Riddhi added. "We've all been there." After a long reflective pause, she continued, "This happens with all of us. Sometimes more pronounced and other times, subtle. Think of every big moment, every presentation we prepare for, every crucial conversation, every leap we need to take in our personal lives. We get nervous. We hesitate. We overthink. We tell ourselves: *What if I mess up? What if they don't understand? What if I'm not good enough?*'

Sagar smiled too. "You know, you sound like you've had this conversation with yourself a hundred times."

"I have," she said, chuckling. "Too many times to count. Where I stopped applying for something. Or didn't speak up. Not because I didn't want it… but because somewhere, I believed people won't value it."

She continued, "You remember, my first panel discussion after returning from that two-year sabbatical? When you commented that I looked like I was about to walk into a firing squad."

Sagar laughed softly.

Riddhi laughed, a dry chuckle that warmed slowly into a smile. "And you suggested that I should imagine the panellists in their boxers."

"I still stand by that," he grinned. "Very effective. Especially when the moderator has a serious moustache."

They laughed, the kind of laugh that loosens something tight in the chest.

Sagar leaned back slightly, letting the car inch forward. The steep curve was coming to an end, the road straightening just enough to breathe.

He continued, "It's all the moments we try to move forward in life, the job switch, the apology we're afraid to make, the confession we hold back, the solo trip we cancel at the last minute, because somewhere inside, the handbrake of fear, doubt, or guilt is still engaged."

"The handbrake doesn't always scream. Sometimes, it's silent. It feels like being cautious. Being rational. Being 'realistic.' But really, it's fear. Or old programming. Or that one failure we never truly made peace with." Riddhi murmured more to herself.

"And sometimes, it's not fear that stops us, it's numbness. The denial that something even needs healing. The quiet suppression of our own potential, just to stay safe. And in that silence, the engine burns, the wheels strain, and the journey halts, without ever making a sound." Sagar added softly.

Riddhi whispered, "And we wonder why we feel stuck."

"It's like trying to accelerate," Sagar said, "with the handbrake still on. The will is there, but the resistance inside us holds us back. We press the pedal hard, showing up, trying hard, but we forget to release the doubts, the fears, the baggage we're dragging around."

The car began to inch forward again. Sagar gently released the handbrake and pressed the accelerator with perfect ease. The vehicle moved ahead, smooth as a breeze.

"And the moment we trust… when we let go of the internal handbrake, we flow. Just like this." He smiled.

The road twisted again, rising like a challenge, but the car responded with grace. It wasn't just about mechanics; it was about the mindset of the driver.

"I've learned something about confidence," Sagar said, shifting gears again. "Confidence isn't the absence of fear; it's the decision to move forward *despite* it."

Riddhi looked out again, the clouds now opening slightly to reveal distant snow-capped peaks. They looked like they belonged to another world altogether.

Sagar glanced at her and nodded, then added, "And the irony is… the car's ready. The road's waiting. It's just the driver who needs to believe."

She turned and smiled, really smiled. Eyes full of knowing. Of arriving.

They parked near the summit and continued on foot, steps crunching over gravel like a soft rhythm. The trees thinned, and the sky opened.

On their way to the lookout, Sagar plucked a tiny yellow wildflower.

Riddhi noticed it instantly.

"Wow, that's beautiful. Yellow's my favourite."

He offered it with a smile. She tucked it behind her ear, her grin quiet and full.

They reached the bend, the old wooden bench overlooking the valley. She brushed fallen leaves from the seat and cleared the bench for Sagar and for herself to sit down, hugging her knees to her chest. He joined her shortly after.

For a while, neither of them spoke.

A soft wind played with her hair. He watched as a single strand lifted, curled, and landed gently on her cheek like a kiss from the wind. She turned to look at him, the horizon reflected in her eyes.

Sagar's heart stumbled.

This was it.

But then, doubt crept in.

What if she says no? What if this ruins what we already have? Maybe what we share is enough. Maybe I shouldn't risk it.

He looked away. But his heart wouldn't sit still.

Then he remembered the uphill curve.

The handbrake.

The truth they had spoken aloud, how love, too, needs courage. How, sometimes, the only thing keeping us from joy is the fear of moving forward.

He realised then:

He had spent too long with his foot hovering over the brake.

But love wasn't built on hesitation. It was built on courage. On release of the handbrake.

And in that moment, he let go.

Quietly. Hands in his jacket pockets. The wind rising gently, like the moment had been waiting for this.

He turned to her, the valley behind him, the sky now painted in soft gold and fire.

Then, with a voice steadier than he expected, he spoke, not rehearsed, not perfect, but real, and looking straight into her eyes, diving deep into them -

"Riddhi, some souls arrive in your life so quietly, you don't even notice when they become home. In you, I've found that. That anchoring. That knowing. I don't want to imagine another mile without you beside me. Through the detours. The speed breakers. The missed turns."

"Riddhi Kalra...will you marry me?"

There was no rush. No dramatic music.

Just the wind. The trees holding their breath. And her eyes, wide, still, shining, hesitated for a moment.

With nervousness in his eyes, he extended his open palm as if inviting her to hold it forever. He could feel the tremble in his breath, like he had laid his whole heart on this quiet clearing, ready to be held or shattered.

Sagar, held his breath tight and sensed Riddhi's first instinct of fear, as if saying -

Should I really say yes? What if this changes everything? What if the girl who promised herself never to fold into someone else's expectations is forgotten?

He recalled – when she had told him, "I don't want to disappear in the name of love. I want companionship, not servitude."

He waited patiently. Letting her reflect on her rearview mirror and handbrakes and immediately noticed when something in her softened, as if she too, had decided to let go of her handbrakes.

She looked at him, really looked. And then stepped forward and gently slipped her hand into his.

Their fingers intertwined quietly, naturally.

For a moment, they just stood like that, holding on.

Then, without a word, she moved closer, her head resting gently on his shoulder.

What began as a touch deepened into an embrace with her arms slipping around him, holding on with tenderness, like she'd been waiting not just for hours or days, but lifetimes.

He pulled her in without hesitation, closer, tighter, trying to gather every moment they'd lost, every smile that had waited, every heartbeat that had lingered in silence..

It wasn't just a hug.

It was a claim. A release. A promise.

Two people.

One road.

Finally arriving… not at a destination, but at a shared beginning.

Reflection: Letting go

Sometimes, it isn't the road that's holding us back. It's the quiet pressure of our own restraint - the handbrake within, subtle, silent, disguised as logic, wrapped in caution.

Maybe we hesitate, not because we don't want to move forward, but because stillness feels safer than uncertainty. Maybe it's denial. Or suppression. Or simply numbness. We forget- no matter how much we press the pedal, the car won't move until we release the brake.

And when we do, the wheels respond. The body aligns. And we begin to flow, not with force, but with trust.

And in that release, we don't just go forward. We come alive.

Chapter 9

The Speed breakers

"Not every slowdown is a setback. Sometimes, it's the universe whispering to pause, reflect and be more present- mindfully."

5:30 a.m.

The alarm buzzed.

Sagar reached for the phone, but for once, didn't hit snooze. Sleep had already stepped aside for memory. The smile came before the stretch, before the yawn, before the light.

Yesterday.

That moment.

That *yes.*

He sat up, the warmth of the quilt falling away, and turned to the window. The sky outside was a soft bruise of violet and ash, dawn still finding its courage.

But in his heart, the sun had already risen.

His fingers grazed the jacket slung on the chair, still carrying the faint perfume of pine, of cold wind, and maybe... of her.

And then he saw it, on the desk.

The wilted yellow wildflower, still intact. The one that Riddhi had tucked behind her ear and later left in the car by mistake. He had carried it to his hotel room, like a prized possession.

Just then, the sharp ring of the intercom snapped him out of his reverie.

It was Riddhi, her voice still laced with sleep, but cheerful and bubbling with a softness that made him smile.

"Good morning. I'm almost ready," she said, a hint of laughter in her tone. "Give me fifteen minutes, and we can leave."

He smiled, rubbing his face with one hand to shake off the last traces of nostalgia and sleep.

"Perfect," he replied. "I'll be ready too."

As he hung up, his heart raced memories of the hilltop moment still echoing inside him, blending with the anticipation of the journey ahead.

They were going back.

Back to the world, yes. But more importantly, forward into a life they were choosing to build together.

He was ready by 6:00 a.m.

Their bags were packed. The keys were returned. The engine purred as Sagar started the car, adjusting the rearview mirror, and entered the GPS coordinates to their destination.

The GPS chimed –

"You are on the fastest route, and you will reach your destination by 8:41 a.m."

Riddhi slid into the passenger seat, her scarf fluttering as she closed the door.

The morning had that crispness only mountain towns know, a blend of cold air and new beginnings.

"You ready?" Sagar asked, his eyes meeting hers, not casually, but searchingly. As if seeking quiet confirmation. Not just for the road ahead, but for everything that came with it.

Riddhi smiled, slow and steady.

"More than I've ever been," she said, and though the words were simple, their meaning wasn't.

She wasn't just ready for the drive down the hills.

She was ready for the ride ahead. For *them.*

They rolled downhill, winding past sleepy trees and shuttered shops. The road stretched ahead, and the silence between them was no longer filled with questions. It was filled with something lighter. *Arrival.*

They were to stop in Dehradun to meet Arjun, Sagar's cousin. The visit had been postponed too long. Arjun had recently been hospitalised after a minor heart episode. Just 34 years old. A fitness freak, a corporate warrior, a TEDx speaker. And yet, his body had made him stop.

And now, he was bedridden.

Paused. Humbled. Interrupted.

The road to Dehradun unspooled before them in lazy curves, a ribbon of tar stretching through sleepy hills and waking villages. The morning sun had now risen fully, casting long shadows of trees across the road. The quiet hum of the engine was the only sound for miles, punctuated occasionally by the honks of the passing vehicles.

Sagar and Riddhi drove mostly in silence, not because there was nothing to say, but because everything had already been said. And understood.

Theirs was a silence that had evolved. No longer heavy with hesitation or the unknown, it had become companionable. Sacred. As though both knew that peace didn't always come with answers, but with presence.

The winding road eventually began to straighten, signalling the outskirts of Dehradun. Familiar landmarks began to appear, rusty signage, petrol pumps, and an old sugarcane juice stall that looked as if it hadn't changed since Sagar's college days.

Just as they approached a fork in the road, marked by a T-point, Sagar instinctively slowed the car. There was a big speed breaker ahead. He had to slow down the speed of the car to almost zero to navigate that speed-breaker.

Riddhi sighed, " I always wonder who designs such humungous speed breakers. They slow down everything, actually bring the car to a full stop."

She further chided, "They should be called – speed stoppers and not speed-breakers."

The car dipped gently over the bump, the tyres murmuring against the road. Sagar was about to accelerate again when they were both startled by a loud horn.

A truck tore through the intersection from the left, its massive body swerving dangerously, engine roaring, horn blaring like an alarm. Dust flew up in its wake.

Sagar instinctively slammed the brakes, and the car came to an immediate halt, as it had already slowed down at the speed breaker.

Had they been just seconds earlier, had Sagar not slowed over at that speed breaker- they would've been directly in the truck's path.

Riddhi let out a breath she hadn't realised she'd been holding.

The air inside the car was suddenly thick- with adrenaline, silence and gratitude.

"That was close," she whispered.

"Too close," Sagar replied, still gripping the wheel tightly.

Riddhi turned to him, eyes wide, the irony not lost on her. "It's like that speed breaker just saved our lives."

He nodded slowly. "It did. Life saver indeed."

She stared ahead at the road, thoughtful. "Funny how I cursed it just moments ago… and now I feel like thanking whoever put it there."

Sagar exhaled, slowly bringing the car back to motion.

"I guess, speed breakers are intentionally placed just before such intersections, to force you into mindfulness. They make you pause, even if you don't want to. And therefore, become instrumental in preventing fatal accidents in the high-risk zones."

Riddhi added, "I now realise that they're not obstacles. They're warnings. They're there because something ahead is dangerous. They force us to notice what we might otherwise ignore."

He looked at her, then at the intersection they had just escaped and took the left turn toward Arjun's house.

It was a modest, ivy-covered building nestled between government quarters and an old park. Arjun's room was on the third floor, its window overlooking a cluster of neem trees and a city slowly waking up.

Arjun was propped up in bed, his face leaner than Sagar remembered, but his smile intact.

"Look who finally decided to show up," he grinned.

Sagar laughed and walked over to hug him gently, careful of all the wires and tubes around him, and settled on the sofa between the window and Arjun's bed. Riddhi sat beside them, warm in her presence.

Still startled by the near miss, Sagar clasped his cousin's hand. "We almost didn't make it to see you today."

Arjun raised an eyebrow. "Traffic?"

Sitting next to Sagar, Riddhi shook her head.

"Speed breaker. T-junction. A truck came out of nowhere. If Sagar hadn't slowed down…"

Sagar finished for her. "We wouldn't be standing here. Just outside, a truck blasted through the intersection. Missed us by seconds."

Arjun's smile faded. His eyes narrowed, not in worry, but in reflection, and he raised an eyebrow. "Seriously?"

Riddhi nodded. "If it wasn't for the speed breaker just before it... We'd probably be in the emergency wing right now."

Arjun exhaled deeply, his features softening.

"Thank God you're okay," he said, his voice low but firm, carrying more weight than the words alone.

He looked between the two of them, his eyes steady.

"Moments like that… they remind you how thin the line really is. I'm just glad life slowed you down, even if just for a second."

Just then, Arjun's mother entered. Sagar and Riddhi stood to greet her and touched her feet. She offered them her blessings, then instructed the house help to bring chai and snacks.

As she sat down, she adjusted the pillow behind her son. Her face was composed but tired, the kind of tired that only comes from loving someone too much for too long.

With concern in his eyes, Sagar asked Arjun and Aunty, "How did this happen? And to you? A person who led such an active life."

"You know, I've watched him push himself for years," she said quietly, looking more towards the window than the room. "Always a new project, a new fitness regime, another target to conquer. Even as a boy, he was always running. First in the playground. Then in the classroom. Later in life… everywhere."

She paused, her voice catching for a moment.

"I told him many times, *'Beta, not every day has to be a race.'* But he'd laugh, say that *'rest'* is for the weak. That if he slowed down, someone else would get ahead."

She looked at Sagar and Riddhi with a sad smile - "And look now. Life stopped him so he could learn to stand still." She quietly wiped her wet eyes.

The room fell silent. Only the soft clinking of teacups being arranged outside broke the silence.

Arjun sighed and, looking out of the window, as if reflecting on his life, slowly said, "I now realise how I ignored the warnings. The little signs. The fatigue, the palpitations, the constant headaches. I thought pushing through was a strength. That speed was the purpose."

He glanced at the ECG monitor beside him.

"Turns out, I just didn't apply the brakes in time. And my body did it for me. Harshly."

Reflecting on his own lifestyle, Sagar leaned forward. "Do you regret it? The hustle?"

Arjun shook his head. "No. But I regret the blindness. I regret not noticing when I needed to pause."

Riddhi, seated near the foot of the bed, spoke softly, her voice laced with quiet insight - "Speed is seductive. It makes you feel invincible."

Sagar added, "It's like what we spoke about yesterday. Handbrakes. Most people keep them pulled-in out of fear. Others never use them at all, and crash."

"Maybe wisdom," Riddhi said, "is knowing when to release and when to hold."

The room held the truth for a moment. Heavy. Real. Needed.

Outside, a koel sang somewhere in the trees. The day, though ordinary in its unfolding, had offered something extraordinary.

Eventually, Arjun broke the silence. "You know, I thought I had everything under control. My calendar, my heart rate, my life plan. But none of it mattered when my body said 'enough.'"

Riddhi reached out and placed a hand on his leg.

"Maybe this isn't a breakdown. Maybe it's your speed breaker. The kind that saves you before the crash."

Arjun looked at her, eyes moist. "I never saw it that way."

Sagar stood, walking over to the window.

"We didn't either. Until today. That jolt, it was terrifying. But it made us more present. It made us respect the journey."

Riddhi and Sagar stayed for nearly two hours. The conversation meandered gently, from childhood stories and shared memories to questions about recovery, change, and what comes next.

They laughed over school pranks, teased Arjun about his fitness freak obsessions, and even discussed his plan to start writing a blog, perhaps on burnout and redefining ambition.

Chai arrived in tall steel tumblers, accompanied by a plate of hot samosas, the kind that crumbled at the edges and burned your tongue if you weren't patient. They sat, sipping slowly, letting the spice and steam fill the room.

Riddhi leaned back, eyes scanning the neem trees outside.

Sagar watched Arjun speak to his mother, noticed the shift, the gentler tone, the humility in his posture, the permission he was now giving himself to be still and heal.

As they prepared to leave, Arjun said, "Thanks for dropping by, Sagar."

Sagar nodded. "Of course, we had to. And I am sorry; it took us this long."

They exchanged a quiet hug. A longer one than usual.

And then Sagar and Riddhi were back in the car.

As they stepped back into the afternoon sun, Riddhi slipped her hand into Sagar's.

"Let's never curse the speed breakers again. "

He smiled. "Never. They're there for a reason. Even if they bring the car to almost a halt."

Silence.

He looked at her and smiled. "Now I can see the role of speed breakers, both on the road and in life. Setbacks, delays, and disruptions often protect us from unseen dangers. What feels like a frustrating halt could be saving us from a head-on collision with something we're not ready for."

As they crossed a similar speed breaker on their way back, this time, Sagar slowed, with full awareness and with grace.

He continued, "They force you to *pay attention.* In life, challenges like heartbreak, illness, or burnout remind us to become more mindful of our choices, our limits, and our relationships."

Looking out of the window and sharing her reflection, Riddhi said, "And talking to Arjun today, made me appreciate that - when we resist necessary pauses, through overwork, emotional denial, or avoidance, we hurt ourselves. Slowing down isn't weakness; it's wisdom."

And after a moment's pause, as if talking to herself, Riddhi said, "Just like speed breakers are *placed* by planners who see what we don't, the delays in life are probably a part of a larger intelligence. Maybe God. Maybe fate. The subconscious. The soul. I don't know. But surely, they're designed *for* us, not *against* us."

And as they drove away, this time at a pace slower, steadier, and deeply aware, the world outside seemed to nod in agreement.

Some journeys begin not when you hit the accelerator. But when you learn the wisdom of the brake.

Reflection: The Gift of Pause

Life isn't built only on the highways we speed through, but in the quiet, unexpected bumps that make us slow down.

And in slowing down, we don't lose time, maybe, we find deeper meaning and realization. Maybe not all delays are detours. Maybe they are prayers in disguise, whispered into our path by a wiser hand than ours. Grace.

Chapter 10

The Fuel Tank

"Renewal is the rhythm behind endurance."

The road from Dehradun to Delhi stretched wide and uneventful, lined with sugarcane fields and the occasional chai stall. The adrenaline of the near accident had faded. The quiet conversation with Arjun had left behind a different kind of stillness, not the kind born from exhaustion, but the kind that invites reflection.

For a long while, they drove in silence. Not the sacred kind this time. Not the heavy kind either. Just... the kind that hangs in the air, leaving you to reflect.

Sagar and Riddhi reached home late Monday evening. As he steered the car through the hushed streets, the moonlight cast silver patterns on the road ahead, as if the stars themselves had paused to witness their return. The night seemed to whisper of the weekend they had just lived, the laughter, the silences, the near-misses, and above all, the quiet vow they had made. Not just to each other, but to something deeper. Soul to soul.

Sagar pulled up outside Riddhi's apartment. The car came to a gentle halt. For a moment, neither moved.

Then, as if the cold itself had nudged them back to the world, they stepped out into the crisp night air. Sagar opened the boot, pulled out Riddhi's bag, and walked around to meet her. The street was quiet. The sky held its breath.

Their eyes met.

Not hurried. Not searching. Just… meeting.

He looked into her, truly into her, as if memorising her presence, as though speaking without words - *I'm here. I see you. Still. Always.*

And Riddhi smiled. That soft, unwavering smile that said everything the lips need not.

A glance. A breath. A silent promise.

"Good night," she whispered. "See you tomorrow."

So ordinary in words. So extraordinary in meaning.

"Good night," he echoed, just as softly. "So... you'll pick me up at 8:30, right?"

"Right. 8:30 sharp."

She gave a playful wave and turned toward her gate.

Sagar stayed where he was, watching her disappear into the building. Only when the door closed behind her did he blink, as if surfacing from a dream. He climbed back into the car, started the engine, and sat there for a beat, smiling to no one in particular.

The past three days unfolded in his mind like a montage.

The mountain air. The confessions. The silences.

The near collision. The yellow wildflower.

The moment.

Complete.

The next morning came quietly.

There was no alarm, no rush.

Just a slow, uncoiling of light through the curtain gaps and a stillness that hung like a gentle hush across the city.

Sagar woke up with the memory of Riddhi's smile still lingering somewhere near his chest, like an ember refusing to die out.

He stretched, yawned, and stayed in bed longer than usual.

For once, the to-do list didn't shout. The emails didn't matter.

Something inside him felt… softer.

He made himself a slow cup of chai, letting the steam rise like a prayer.

Then sat by the window, watching the morning stir to life. A fruit vendor's call, the faint rumble of a milk van, birds making music out of ordinary sounds.

He got ready without hurrying, not as a checklist but as a rhythm.

At 8:25, he locked the door behind him, called the lift, and, mindfully, smiled and greeted the neighbours inside.

Downstairs, he stopped to chat with the security guard.

"How's your knee now, Bhaiya?"

"Better, Sir. Thank you for asking," came the smiling response.

By 8:30, Riddhi pulled up. Her face was radiant with sleep-softened calm and the quiet satisfaction of routine.

"You slept well?" she asked, reading his energy with practised ease.

He smiled back. "Surprisingly, yes. Still carrying some mountain peace in me, I think."

They drove in easy conversation - office, life, chai flavours- until they reached their building.

But the moment they entered, they felt it.

The air was different. Heavy. Gloomy.

Sagar caught the eye of a colleague passing by. "What's going on?"

A pause.

Then the words that followed struck like ice:

"Vineet passed away. Saturday night. Heart attack."

The world seemed to contract.

Vineet? The 32-year-old cheerful guy. The award-winning performer. The "Yes, I got it!" guy who made success look like a morning jog.

"Survived by his wife and two young children," someone added quietly.

The office had arranged a short prayer meet. A two-minute silence.

Everyone stood, heads bowed, but hearts loudly unsettled.

After the prayer meet, as colleagues began drifting back into routine, Sagar lingered in the corridor outside the conference room, his eyes unintentionally pulled toward the far corner of the floor.

Vineet's desk. It sat there, untouched. Still.

Like it, too, hadn't yet accepted the news.

A soft paperweight held down a few loose pages.

A framed photo of Vineet with his family, his wife and two children, smiling on a beach, forever captured in a moment of sunlit laughter. Two coffee mugs. One chipped. One half-washed. A yellow sticky note on the edge of the monitor:

"Take Dad for a check-up. Don't delay."

Bold letters. Underlined twice. As if urgency itself had been begging to be heard.

Sagar stood motionless.

That note...

It wasn't just ink. It was a mirror. All the things we plan to do tomorrow. Assuming there will be one. There was also a to-do list scribbled on a whiteboard near Vineet's chair, half-erased.

One item had a star beside it:

"Q3 Presentation – 80% done."

Sagar's throat tightened.

Eighty percent.

And now, it would stay that way. Forever. No one would ever know how he planned to end that slide deck. Or what insights he would've added. Or what his voice would have sounded like presenting it.

The desk felt like a pause button hit too hard.

Sagar couldn't stop thinking about Arjun. Auntie's tired voice. The wires. The monitor. The stillness.

And now this – Vineet.

What was this invisible weight we are carrying?

The chase. The speed. The unshed tears.

What was it all costing?

Sagar walked back slowly, his hands in his pockets, head lowered.

He couldn't shake the feeling in his chest, something between sadness and shame.

We all believe it happens to others. That somehow, we're untouchable. Too young. Too fit. Too important. As if the body takes note of ambition and grants immunity.

Or we become too indifferent, thinking, whatever has to happen will happen, so why bother now? Or can I really do something about it? Not really. That quiet indifference. Either because of denial… or fatigue… or the comforting lie that there's still time.

We silence the signs - the skipped meals, the shallow sleep, the rising anger, the breathlessness on stairs that didn't used to wind us. We tell ourselves it's just a phase, just pressure, just temporary.

Until one day, the body stops asking politely and makes the pause *permanent.*

Sagar looked around the office as if seeing it anew. The fluorescent lights. The sound of rapid keystrokes. The murmur of meetings. Everything moved on, like life always does.

But one desk, just one, remained still. And in that stillness, was the loudest message of all.

Over lunch that day, the group sat subdued: Riddhi, Sagar, Aishwarya, and Rohan.

The food was there. But appetite had left.

Rohan spoke first. Softly. "It's shocking. But honestly… not surprising anymore. There has been a discernible trend of heart attacks and more people dying from them than ever before. Latest statistics from the Indian Heart Association state that in India, 50% of heart attacks in men happen under the age of 50, and 25% before 40."

He continued wistfully, "Seemingly fit people dying of lifestyle disorders."

And then, as an afterthought, he added thoughtfully, "Every 1 in 4 dying of a heart attack!"

Aishwarya nodded. "And Indians develop these heart conditions nearly a decade earlier than in the West. It's terrifying."

Rohan leaned in. "And who's the culprit – we! Our lifestyle! Poor sleep. Anxiety about job loss. Stress over being 'enough'. When do we know it's too much? When do we stop?"

Silence. No one answered. Because the questions were bigger than the table they sat around.

Vineet's voice echoed in Sagar's head, his laugh, his relentless drive, his awards.

And now… gone.

Gone with no warning.

Leaving behind a wife, two children, and an office full of unread Slack messages.

The lunch ended quietly. No coffee runs. No memes passed across phones. Only silence.

By evening, things at work began returning to the default pace. Projects resumed. Deadlines resurfaced. The news, like the man, had vanished into the background.

On their drive back home, the car rolled in a heavier silence.

The dashboard glowed softly.

Fuel low.

Riddhi noticed first and turned into a fuel station. They got out, refilled the tank, and checked the tyres. Routine.

As they climbed back in, Sagar stared at the dashboard a second longer.

"The car knows," he said softly. "When it's time to pause. To refuel. To be taken care of."

He turned to Riddhi. "But us? We don't. We drive through headaches, fatigue, and tension. We ignore the signs. We think pushing harder will fix it."

Riddhi didn't interrupt. She knew this moment needed its own breath.

Sagar went on. "Is a weekend get-away enough? A month's vacation? How often do we check in with ourselves? Really check in. Where's our fuel meter?"

A long silence filled the car.

Outside, a tree rustled. Inside, something softened.

The hum of the engine settled into a quiet lull as the city lights blurred past, gentle and golden. The moment held a certain kind of stillness, not empty, but expectant.

And then, softly, almost as if speaking to herself, Riddhi broke the silence.

"Sagar," she began, her voice low and reflective, "do you know what my favourite part of the day is?"

He turned his head slightly but didn't speak. He knew she wasn't asking for a reply, just space to unfold.

"It's not something grand," she continued. "It's those quiet minutes before the world fully wakes up… just me and the morning."

Her gaze drifted toward the windshield, as if it had turned into a screen playing a memory.

"I wake up around five," she said, a small smile brushing her lips. "The house is silent. Not just quiet, but truly still. Even the clocks seem to tick more gently. I change into my walking shoes, and step outside just as the first blush of dawn begins to touch the sky."

Sagar listened, the image forming vividly in his mind.

"The air at that hour…" she breathed in, as though reliving it. "It's cold, it's alive. Crisp. It brushes your cheeks like a whisper, like life itself saying: 'I'm still here.' I walk slowly at first, letting my body remember its rhythm. And then, as I walk, I begin to feel... lighter."

She paused.

"And then I reach Central Park under the old peepal tree at the edge of the park, its roots running deep, like a grandparent holding the earth together. I sit down on the stone bench beneath it, close my eyes, and just… breathe."

There was something sacred in the way she said it. As if breathing, in that moment, became an act of devotion.

"When I inhale deeply," she said softly, "it feels like I'm not just drawing air into my lungs, but light. Healing. Clarity. As if every breath repairs what the day before has frayed."

She paused, her gaze unfixed now, as if seeing something far beyond the windshield.

"But it's the exhale," she continued, her voice slowing to a murmur, "where the real magic happens."

Sagar listened, closer now, not just with ears, but with attention.

"When I breathe out," she said, "I feel the tension leave, not just my shoulders, not just my chest… but from deep inside. With every breath out, I feel something being peeled off me, layers of noise, weight, pressure, expectation."

She paused, as if reliving the sensation.

"It's like every cell, every little atom of my being, melts into something softer. Surreal. A complete diffusion with the stillness. As though I stop being solid for a moment and become air… mist… a quiet ripple on the surface of a still lake."

Sagar imagined it: her seated beneath the peepal tree, the wind gently grazing her skin, her breath folding into silence.

"When I exhale," she whispered, "I'm no longer trying to hold anything together. Not my body. Not my identity. Not even my thoughts. I just… let go."

She turned toward him.

"And in that letting go, I don't feel small. I feel… infinite. Like I've dissolved into the universe. Like I've slipped between the seconds and become part of something timeless."

A beat passed.

"That's the peace I can't describe," she added. "Not joy, not calm, not even silence. Just, weightlessness."

She smiled now, gently.

"And when I whisper my affirmations, - *I am calm. I am healing*, it's like the cells in my body listen. I imagine them waking up, stretching after a long sleep, smiling. Rejuvenated with the energy from the divine and merging into the cosmos."

Sagar felt the words settle into the space between them like a hush that wasn't empty, but full. Full of everything he didn't know he needed to hear.

She smiled, not at him, but at the thought.

"The birds are just beginning to stir by then. Their chirping isn't background noise, it's music. A kind of morning orchestra that doesn't ask for applause. And as the first rays of sunlight break through the canopy, the whole world feels like it's been dipped in gold."

Sagar was silent. Moved.

"And that," she said finally, placing her hand gently over her heart, "that is my pit stop. My fuel pump. Not once a year. Not once a week. Every day. And in that moment, my breath, my silence, my sunrise, it fills me in ways nothing else can."

She turned to him now, her eyes soft but clear.

"No resort in the hills. No five-star weekend getaway. Nothing compares to those 45 minutes of being *with myself.* That's when I know, no matter how chaotic the day gets, I've returned to centre. I've filled the tank."

Sagar said nothing. But something inside him stirred.

Longing, maybe.

Hope, perhaps.

He wasn't ready. But he was curious. He glanced at her again. She wasn't trying to convince him. She wasn't selling anything. She was just… living it.

And that authenticity carried a kind of quiet gravity that pulled him in.

He exhaled, slowly, like someone unlearning the need to always be composed.

Then, turning slightly toward her, he spoke, his voice low, uncertain, but real.

"Riddhi… will you take me along tomorrow morning?"

The question hung in the air, weightier than it sounded.

Because it wasn't just about a walk.

It was a confession. A surrender. A hope.

Riddhi turned, her eyes lighting up in surprise and something else - pride, maybe. Or tenderness.

"You?" she teased, eyebrows raised. "You'll have to wake up at 5:00 a.m., Mr. Sagar Sachdeva. No snoozing. No excuses."

He chuckled, rubbing the back of his neck. "I know. I know."

"Are you sure?" she asked again, this time gently.

He nodded.

"I'm not saying I'll float through it. I'll probably grumble. I might curse the birds. I may walk like a zombie for the first twenty minutes. But…"

"I want to try. I think… It's time. To start choosing differently."

A silence followed.

But it wasn't awkward.

It was full.

Reflection: Renewal

That breathlessness on the stairs, the migraine that keeps returning, the irritability without cause, the sleep that leaves us tired, the joy that feels out of reach - these are not just passing discomforts. They are quiet blinkers on the dashboard of our life - signals we often ignore.

Until one day, the whisper turns into a scream. And the journey halts, not because we were too fast, but because we kept running on empty.

Maybe we need to remind ourselves the wisdom of: Pause. Breathe. Re-tune. Re-fuel. Because the true journey isn't outwards, but inwards, towards a self we've long forgotten to sit with.

Chapter 11

The Chosen Lane

"Regret is a thief that robs present to mourn yesterday's wisdom."

The alarm buzzed.

4:30 a.m.

It sounded alien. Unforgiving. Like a distant siren pulling him out of a dream he couldn't remember.

Sagar stirred. Disoriented. His hand flailed for the phone before he even opened his eyes. When he finally did, the numbers on the screen glowed like a dare.

Where was he?

And then, it all came back in a flood.

Arjun.

Vineet.

The pit stops.

The late-night conversation.

And Riddhi's words, etched in the quiet space of his mind.

"Nothing compares to those 45 minutes of being with myself… I've returned to the centre. I've filled the tank."

He groaned. Loudly. The room was dark, the sheets warm, the pillow a comforting weight beneath his head. The idea of peeling himself out of bed felt absurd. Even cruel.

He closed his eyes again, just for a second.

A whisper rose:

"You tried. That's what matters. Go back to sleep."

But then another voice followed, quieter, firmer, not Riddhi's, not anyone's, his own. One he hadn't heard in a long time.

"What if she's right? What if there's magic waiting?"

He sat up halfway, the blanket clinging to him like resistance itself. The cold slapped his skin. His body screamed for mercy. His muscles argued. His past habits begged.

Go back to bed.

It's too early.

This isn't you.

This is her thing. Not yours.

But then, he saw her. Not in the room, but in his mind. Riddhi, under the peepal tree, breathing. Melting. Dissolving. Becoming mist. Her words echoing - not as advice, but as an invitation.

A pause.

Sagar swung his legs off the bed.

Cold floor.

Harsh air.

Regret rising.

He sat there for a full minute, elbows on his knees, hands hanging limp. Eyes shut.

He could still crawl back in. Pull the blanket over his head. Sleep till seven. Or eight. Blame the alarm. Pretend he forgot.

But he didn't.

Instead, he stood. Slowly. Reluctantly. Like someone pulling away from a familiar embrace.

He fumbled for his track pants, his hoodie, and slipped on his shoes like a child learning to walk again. Everything about it felt awkward, unnatural. But it was a start.

He stepped out.

The hallway was dark. The world- silent. He paused by Riddhi's door, its light still off. Maybe she was still getting ready. Maybe she hadn't even woken up yet. Maybe he had time to back out.

He closed his eyes, listening.

No birds yet.

No signs of magic.

Just air and quiet and the thump of his own hesitant heartbeat.

He took a deep breath. Then another. They didn't yet feel sacred. Not yet like light or healing, or dissolving. But they were his. For now, they were enough.

The door across the hallway creaked open.

Riddhi emerged, wrapped in a light shawl, her hair tied loosely, her face glowing, not with makeup or performance, but with presence.

She stopped when she saw him.

And smiled.

Not wide. Not surprised. Just... warm.

As if she'd known he would come.

He stood there awkwardly, rubbing his temple. "Told you I'd grumble."

Riddhi chuckled softly, stepping beside him.

"Yes," she said, opening the front door slowly, "but you also said you'd try."

The morning air rushed in like a silent applause.

Cold. Alive. Whispering.

Sagar exhaled. A real, honest exhale.

And then, without a word, they stepped out together, into the half-light, into the stillness, into the possibility of becoming air.

The path was dimly lit, painted in shades of steel and blue by the fading night. The trees stood tall, silhouettes of silence. The road ahead curved gently, like an invitation that didn't push, only offered.

Sagar walked beside Riddhi, hands in his pockets, shoulders hunched against the morning chill. He noticed how she didn't rush. She wasn't power walking. She moved as though she had all the time in the world.

And that alone was disorienting.

He tried matching her pace, but something inside him wanted to speed up. Finish it. Tick it off. Like a task. A goal. A thing to be achieved.

But this wasn't that.

They didn't speak. Not because there was tension, but because there was no need.

Sagar's footsteps crunched lightly against gravel. The sound - oddly satisfying.

His breath was visible in the cold air, fogging out in little clouds.

His mind, on the other hand, restless.

What am I doing here?

How long will this take?

I could've gotten another hour of sleep.

What if nothing happens?

He caught himself and sighed. The mind never ran out of things to say.

Then, he glanced at Riddhi again. Her face was soft. Her gaze calm. Not smiling, just present. There. Rooted.

They reached the park just as the sky began to shift, a faint line of gold bleeding through the horizon. The peepal tree stood ahead, majestic and still, as if it had never moved in centuries. As if it had seen every version of dawn.

Riddhi led him to the stone bench beneath it and sat down. He hesitated.

"Just sit," she whispered. "Don't try to *do* anything. Not yet."

He obeyed, cautiously lowering himself. The stone was cold. The ground smelled of dew and crushed leaves.

"What now?" he asked, half-joking.

"Now... we breathe," Riddhi said.

The expressions flickered across Sagar's face, confused, amused, and slightly intrigued, as if to say, *What's the big deal about breathing? Don't we do it all the time?*

She smiled - a knowing, unhurried smile. And then, with compassion in it, and a touch of mischief too – she said,

"Breath is not just air, Sagar. It's the moment we finally sit with ourselves, not running, not reaching, just being. When we breathe with awareness, we begin to see ourselves… every cell rising and falling, expanding and softening. It's as if the body remembers its rhythm, and the mind stops pretending to be somewhere else. In that pause in between each inhale and exhale, the 'us' that is tangled in noise begins to dissolve… and what's left is something quieter, vaster. A trace of the consciousness we're made of."

She closed her eyes and inhaled. He tried to copy her. Closed his eyes. Sat still.

Within seconds, he felt everything.

The ache in his lower back.

The itch near his eyebrow.

The way one sock was scrunched under his heel.

The constant hum of thoughts, flashing like headlines in his brain.

This is stupid.

I don't think I'm doing it right.

Should I be breathing deeper?

What if I fall asleep sitting up?

Still, he stayed.

There was something grounding about the silence.

The occasional birdcall.

A distant bark.

The wind brushing gently against his cheeks.

He exhaled.

Then inhaled.

Held it.

Exhaled again.

He opened one eye to peek at Riddhi.

Still as stone.

But not frozen.

Alive, somehow.

He closed his eyes again.

This time, he tried listening, to the rustle of leaves overhead, to the rise and fall of his own breath, to the stillness between sounds.

And then… something softened.

Not much.

Just enough.

He didn't dissolve. He didn't melt into air. He didn't have a revelation or hear the universe whisper back.

But he felt a pause.

A space between thoughts.

A brief, flickering silence inside him.

And in that silence, for the first time in a long time... he didn't feel pulled in ten directions.

Just here.

Just this.

Just now.

When he opened his eyes again, the sun had cracked through the clouds, spilling light over the tree like liquid fire. Everything shimmered- the grass, the bark, the quiet.

Riddhi looked over at him and smiled, not asking how it went.

He didn't say anything either.

But he looked up at the sky, his breath calmer now, and whispered:

"I think I get it. Not all of it... but something."

Riddhi nodded. "That's enough for today."

They rose quietly and began walking back.

And for the first time in a long time, Sagar didn't feel the urge to check his phone. Or rush. Or plan his day.

He just walked.

One step at a time.

Sagar looked at his watch. 7:00 a.m. sharp.

They were back by 7:00 am!

He let out a breath, surprised. Normally, this was when his alarm rang. This was when he'd groggily pull himself out of bed, snooze once or twice, and then drag his unwilling body to the bathroom.

But today, his legs, though not used to early walking, felt stretched and awake. His breath moved through his chest with ease. Even his mind, usually foggy and fragmented at this hour, felt clear. Grounded.

He felt like his body had clicked into place.

Like some tuning fork had struck deep within his system.

He was alert, not in the hyperactive, coffee-induced way, but in a *calm readiness.*

For the first time in weeks, getting ready for the office didn't feel like a burden. It felt like a continuation. A gentle step forward, not a reluctant push.

By 8:00 a.m., he was at the breakfast table. He picked up his coffee, still steaming, and took a slow sip.

And in that pause, he realized, this morning hadn't changed everything. But it had changed *something.*

And that something… felt like a beginning.

He picked up Riddhi right on time, and soon they were weaving through the morning rush. Outside, the city had begun its daily orchestra, buses jostled for space, autos zigzagged with practised impatience, and horns rose like the heartbeat of a place always in a hurry. As they neared the Sector 48 exit, the familiar frenzy thickened - cars nudged into tighter gaps, bikes snaked between mirrors, and the road pulsed with a restless urgency, as if everyone was trying to outrun time itself.

They approached the signal near Sector 48. Five lanes ahead. Twenty cars across. Sagar, by habit, veered confidently into the one he thought would move fastest.

The timer at the signal was blinking

110 ...109....

As they were waiting for the signal to turn green, Sagar rested his elbow on the window and looked out. His gaze danced across the other vehicles stopped beside them.

To their left, a modest WagonR. A middle-aged man was at the driving seat, his wife beside him scrolling through her phone, their teenage son in the backseat staring out, earphones on.

Behind them, a taxi, one of those new electric sedans. A driver in uniform sat stiffly behind the wheel while a sharply dressed executive in the back flipped through the *Business Standard.* Numerous other cars with office goers lined up behind them.

And then came a striking black Mercedes, purring softly to their right. The car was a beauty - sleek, polished, intimidating. But what caught Sagar's eye wasn't its form. It was the solitude in it. A chauffeur sat behind the wheel. And in the back seat sat a lone figure in a crisp white shirt, talking softly on the phone.

Sagar turned sideways-

"Isn't it odd," he murmured, "how the most expensive cars are often driven by someone else?"

Riddhi raised an eyebrow.

"I mean," he continued, referring to Mercedes to their right, "you'd think the pleasure of driving such a machine would belong to the person who owns it. The guy in the back probably spent half his life dreaming of that car. Now that he owns it, someone else drives it. Think of it, it's the drivers who get to feel the power, the control... the thrill. The ones who sit in the back, they're just… passengers. It's strange, isn't it?"

Riddhi followed his gaze and raised an eyebrow, curious and piqued.

"I am not sure," he said slowly, eyes still on the road ahead. "But sometimes I feel ambition plays tricks on us. You chase something for years, sometimes for your family, sometimes just for yourself. And when you finally get there… it doesn't feel like you thought it would."

He paused before continuing.

"By then, the people you were doing it for, your parents, your kids, your partner, they've learned to live without you around. Your absence became a routine, and now your presence feels... optional. Or maybe you've changed so much in the chase, you don't even know how to enjoy what you worked so hard for."

His gaze wandered to a passing luxury car.

"Ever noticed how rarely you see families together in those high-end cars? Maybe because everyone has their own car…. " Sagar said very softly.

"Or maybe... because they've stopped having shared destinations," added Riddhi.

Pause.

"Maybe that's the real cost of ambition," she said quietly. "Not just the sleepless nights or the missed meals... but the drifting. The growing apart. We chase dreams thinking we're doing it *for* someone, but somewhere along the way, we stop noticing *with* whom we were meant to share them."

She glanced sideways at him, her eyes more introspective now.

He added, "And the strange thing is… the world keeps applauding - promotions, possessions, milestones. But no one claps when you choose to slow down and sit at the dinner table with your family. Or take a walk with your parents. Or just… stay."

The light continued counting down.

60...59...

"Maybe that's what ambition does to us. It makes us chase things, thinking they'll make us feel alive. But once we have them... we don't even hold the steering wheel anymore."

He paused, then added, "This morning, when I was sitting under that tree, I remembered what it felt like to breathe without chasing. To just be."

Riddhi smiled slightly, waiting.

He went on. "Out here, in traffic, all I want is to get ahead. Find the faster lane. Escape the wait. But under that tree… I didn't feel like I had to *go* anywhere. I felt so…so… *complete*."

"You know what else I realized?" he said. "Back there, I wasn't multitasking. I wasn't trying to win. And for the first time in a long time… I felt present. Alive. Like I wasn't being driven by time. I was… with it."

Riddhi looked ahead, her voice quiet. "And now?"

He smiled softly. "Now I can feel the rush coming back. This lane. That lane. Getting late. Getting there. As if I am being swept away by this rush."

Just then, 5…4…3…2….1….GO……the light turned green.

The other lanes beside them surged forward, cars zipping past like impatient bees freed from a hive.

But their lane didn't budge.

The first car in their lane, an old Dzire, stuttered. Then stalled.

Riddhi grinned. "No way. Of all the lanes…"

The horns began, that familiar Gurgaon chorus. The driver in front waved sheepishly as he struggled to get his car started, and after a couple of seconds, finally managed to start his car.

Sagar leaned forward. "Classic. Always happens when something important is lined up at work."

He shifted gears, tension rising again. That old current.

"You know," she said, "you sat through discomfort this morning. Through itchiness. Restlessness. You didn't run. You stayed."

He looked at her, caught off guard.

"And maybe," she continued, "that's the practice. Not just under a tree. But here. In traffic. In meetings. In delays. Choosing presence over reaction."

He sank back into his seat.

"That's harder than it sounds."

Riddhi chuckled. "We picked the best lane with the information we had. That's all anyone can do".

He shook his head, frustrated. "Still feels like I made the wrong choice." Sagar shifted gears, still a little rattled. But he didn't say much. And Riddhi, sensing it, stayed silent too.

As they got back into the rhythm of the drive, Riddhi said, "It is so difficult to constantly be mindful that the key isn't to always take the right decisions in life. It's to stop punishing ourselves for not knowing what we couldn't have known better *then*."

He shot her a sideways glance. "You sound like you've said that to yourself many times."

She smiled. "I have."

He grinned. "Me too. You know my first car was the most basic model of the Maruti Alto. And then I kept upgrading. Not because I *needed* to, but because I *wanted* to. Hatchback to sedan to SUV. And in that pursuit, I kept switching jobs. Each job change meant deciding on choosing a new lane… a bigger car… a better house. I was chasing speed. Each job came with a fatter cheque …bigger responsibility….and that gave me a high."

He paused.

"But little did I see *then* that I was choosing the wrong lanes. I didn't look at the company's culture. Or whether the work made me feel alive. All I saw were numbers. In the offer letter. In the pay cheque. In my bank account."

"And then?" she asked gently.

"And then I started waking up tired. Toxic bosses. Unrealistic deadlines. Sleepless nights. Dreading Mondays.

I was no longer the driver. Just someone being driven by targets and goals. A backseat passenger in my own story."

Riddhi looked straight ahead.

Nodding slowly, her voice quiet. "You're right. We keep switching lanes, hoping the next one's faster, smoother, more rewarding."

He looked at her, and then back at the soon approaching office building.

"What if it's not about choosing the fastest lane," he said, "but choosing the one where we're *willing to be fully present.* Even when it stalls. Even when it's slow."

They sat in reflective silence.

Softly, Riddhi added, "We're taught to plan so much, degrees, jobs, finances, even relationships. But no one teaches us how to *choose.* How to live with the weight of a decision... or the silence of the ones we didn't make."

They watched the cars around them, each carrying a story, a purpose, a past. Some moved quickly, others hesitated. But all were moving.

And maybe that was the point.

Not to find the perfect lane.

Not to always make the fastest move.

But to own the choices we make.

Riddhi glanced at him, her voice almost a whisper.

"So… what if we stopped chasing the perfect lane? And just chose one. With intention. With heart."

Riddhi smiled, watching his hands on the steering wheel.

"Then maybe," he said, "we'd finally start driving again… not just through traffic, but through life, awake, aware… and side by side."

And as the city moved around them in all its rush and rhythm, he reached over and placed his hand gently over hers, not as a gesture of arrival, but as a quiet promise to stay present for the journey ahead.

Reflection: The chosen lane

We look back often at the lanes we took and the ones we left behind.

The job we accepted… or didn't. The stocks we bet on… or hesitated to. The house we bought… or let go. The hand we held… or walked past.

Life offers no perfect choices, only moments. We chose with the heart we had then, and that was enough.

Peace begins when we stop questioning the past and start honouring every choice as a step toward becoming.

Chapter 12

Co-Passengers

"Some passengers never leave. They just switch seats, from beside you to inside you."

It was a Friday. Only been three days since the new ritual!

But to Sagar, the past three days had felt quietly significant. Each morning, before the city stirred, he rose and joined Riddhi under the soft pre-dawn sky. It wasn't easy; his body still protested the early hour, his mind often wandered during meditation, and the previous day, the urge to stay under the covers nearly won.

But something had shifted. He was beginning to get the hang of it. His steps felt a little less reluctant, his breath a little steadier. The silence, once awkward, now felt familiar, like a language he was slowly learning to speak.

It wasn't a transformation. Not yet. But it was a start.

Sagar was driving today. Usually, Riddhi would've a happy disposition on Friday evenings, would be humming a tune, or playfully announcing "Thank God It's Friday!" like it was a national celebration. But today was different. There was a stillness in her, an air of quiet withdrawal, as she sat beside Sagar in the car, eyes lost somewhere beyond the road.

He noticed it almost instantly. Her silence wasn't empty; it was full. Full of something she wasn't saying.

As they pulled out of the office parking lot and the engine came alive, Sagar turned slightly toward her and asked, in a voice as gentle as dusk, "Everything okay?"

Riddhi nodded but then hesitated. Her voice, when it came, was heavy, like a stone carefully carried for too long.

"It's Papa's fourth death anniversary tomorrow."

Sagar didn't speak. He didn't need to. Some silences are better held than filled.

Riddhi looked out through the windshield, not really seeing the present.

"Time just flies by, and life moves on," she said softly. "But some moments… they don't move at all. They stay lodged in your memory like a loop. Playing over and over again, every time you think of someone."

There was a tremor in her voice. But also warmth, like the kind of ache that comes with love too deep to forget.

"You know, Papa was that one person... rock solid behind me," she said. "Always showing me the way. Always believing I could do more, be more. And when I did… he'd be the loudest one cheering in the crowd."

"And then, there were school annual days… I remember every single one. I'd be on stage receiving some award, and there he would be, front row, already standing before they even called my name, clapping like the world had just crowned a Queen. His eyes… I can never forget those eyes.

Like I was his most prized possession. Like I was enough, more than enough."

She chuckled softly, but her eyes brimmed.

"And once I fell from the monkey bars and split open my knee… I was crying so loudly in the doctor's clinic. The doctor said I'd need stitches. Papa stayed beside me till the injection went in, and then… he quietly stepped outside. Later, I found out he couldn't bear to see me in pain. He cried too. Outside. Alone."

Sagar glanced at her and saw the moisture quietly collecting near the edges of her eyes.

"And then there were these evening walks... he would take me to Central Park in our colony. There were some stepped structures there, kind of architectural steps. I would climb to the highest one and jump… right into his arms."

Riddhi paused.

"Never for even a moment did I doubt I'd fall. He'd stand there, arms wide open, and I'd leap like it was the most natural thing in the world. And every time I landed in his arms, he'd hold me tight, spin me a little, and just squeeze me into his chest."

Sagar could feel her heart travel backward, reliving a frame of time that still beat with life.

Riddhi smiled, lost.

"That moment… that was the world. That was safety. That was… divinity."

Riddhi's voice cracked ever so slightly. "So much love. So much of it that it felt like my heart would explode holding it all."

A hush settled over the car, one of those rare silences that feels sacred, like a prayer being said without words.

"And you know," she added after a pause, "his love wasn't just for me. It radiated outward. To all our cousins… the neighbour's kids… the cleaner's children… even some uncle's uncle's kids no one really remembered." She let out a soft chuckle through the emotion. "He treated each of them like they were the most important person in the world. Asking riddles, ruffling their hair, and showering them with praise like they'd just won the Nobel Prize."

She paused, her eyes shimmering with the weight of memory.

"And it wasn't just us kids. His friends, his colleagues, even the milkman, everyone had a space in his world. Our drawing room could barely contain the love that poured in on his birthday, or Diwali, or any random Sunday when people dropped by just to feel his presence."

Another pause. The hum of the car filled the quiet.

When Riddhi spoke next, her voice was softer, as though the words themselves needed gentling.

"He was everywhere. In everyone's life. The first person his friends called in need. The first to receive a box of sweets when there was something to celebrate. The one everyone turned to for advice. And he never showed up halfway, he came with everything he had. His presence, his energy, that unmistakable warmth… it filled the room like sunlight."

She fell quiet again. Words weren't needed. Some love stories are too large for language.

The car slowed to a stop. The sudden honk of a scooter jerked her attention back. They were at a red light, buses jostling, pedestrians rushing past, a balloon vendor weaving between cars, his colors bobbing like strange, joyful memories.

Then after a pause she said,

"You know, it was he who taught me to drive. We had a white Fiat Premier. Those elegant old cars with their vintage charm and steering-column gear shift. We'd go out early mornings, with him sitting next to me, calm, patient, correcting my hand, gently pushing the brake when I forgot."

"Now that I come to think of it, he was my first co-passenger." Riddhi's eyes grew glassy.

"And then… he was my last." Her voice dropped.

Sagar looked at her quietly.

"We were both in the rear seat. But this time, on our final ride together, we weren't heading out for a drive. The special vehicle, was headed to the cremation ground."

Riddhi's voice cracked, but she didn't hold it back.

"He was quiet, unnaturally quiet. Still. So was I. Numb."

She looked away, drew a deep breath, and whispered, "It was the last time I held him. The final time I said goodbye."

"And then, on the way back, there I was. In that same special bus. The same one we both rode together for our last ride, except this time, I was alone. Just me. My co-passenger had completed his journey."

They sat in silence again, but this time, the air wasn't heavy. It was sacred.

"It was four years ago. I still remember the morning of the cremation," Riddhi said, her voice breaking into a whisper.

"I performed every ritual myself. Every last farewell, with these hands. Papa made me promise, months before he passed, that I would do it all… even the rituals that tradition reserved for a son."

She paused, then said with quiet resolve:

"And I did. I lit the pyre."

A breath. A silence.

"With the same hands he once held as we crossed the road. The same hands that made him Father's Day cards every year, all shaky lines and crooked hearts, 'Best Papa in the World.' Those same hands… I used to set his body on fire."

Her eyes shimmered, but she didn't look away this time.

"To turn him into ash. Into white, washed-out nothingness."

Riddhi swallowed hard. She couldn't say more. Her eyes said it all.

Her tears rolled slowly, like each one carrying a lifetime.

"But maybe… maybe that's what love is," Sagar added very softly with reverence.

"The form goes. The body, the voice, the smile…. All of it disappears. But something stays behind. Something formless. Something so deep, it becomes part of you."

Riddhi looked at him, her tears still rolling. But now, they carried understanding.

Very gently, Sagar placed his hand over hers.

"I think that's what eternal love is, we're not meant to hold on to the *form*. We carry their essence. That's what lives."

Sagar continued, more quietly now, as if the words were forming from somewhere beyond him.

"From form to formlessness… that's where love proves it's real. When you can no longer see them, but you still *feel* them. When they stop sitting beside you and start living *inside* you."

Riddhi looked out at the dusky sky, her voice low, almost like she was speaking to herself more than anyone else.

"You know… we plan so much. Careers. Promotions. Vacations. Retirement goals. We mark our calendars with deadlines, targets, and milestones. But no one, no one ever plans for *that* ride. The final one. The one to the cremation ground. And yet, that's the *only* ride guaranteed."

She took a breath, then turned slightly toward Sagar, her tone even gentler now. "Have you ever wondered… who'll be our co-passengers on that final ride? Who'll sit in that last vehicle with us? The ones who will drop everything, rearrange their lives for a day, to walk that final stretch with you…"

He paused.

"Our family. Our friends. Our people." He added.

"And yet," Riddhi said, her voice trembling, "how present are we in their lives… really present? Do we spend enough time with them? Or are we too caught up rushing toward invisible finish lines to even notice if someone's falling behind? Do we know what's really happening in the lives of the ones we love? Or are we just... co-existing?"

He exhaled, thinking of his own mother.

"We obsess over who'll sit next to us in business class. But do we ever stop to think who'll sit next to us on that slow, quiet, final ride?"

A silence lingered in the car, still, thoughtful, sacred.

Riddhi continued, "And here's the thing. When Papa died... it wasn't just the rituals or the fire. It was the presence of people who came. Old friends. Neighbours. Colleagues. Even a teacher of mine. People who didn't have to be there but chose to be. Because in his life, he had *been there* for them. Fully. Authentically. Genuinely."

Sagar looked into her glassy eyes. "That's what lingers ... the imprint you leave on people's hearts."

Riddhi remained still, absorbing every word, and another tear gently rolled down her cheek.

Then, after a long pause, she smiled faintly, "And such co-passengers...with indelible imprints... never leave. They move from the front seat to the back seat... and then slowly, quietly... they enter our heart. They become the rhythm of your kindness, the voice in your silence, the courage behind your leap. They stop riding *with* you and start riding *within* you."

Sagar looked at her, not with sympathy, but with something far deeper. Something that didn't try to fix the ache but chose to stay beside it.

Very softly, like a whisper in twilight, he offered his shoulder to Riddhi.

For a fleeting moment, she searched his eyes, not for answers, but for anchoring. And then, slowly, tenderly, she rested her head on his shoulder.

It wasn't dramatic.

It wasn't loud.

But in that one gesture, so still, so human, so impossibly gentle, an unspoken promise was made.

A promise carved not with words, but with presence.

The kind of presence that doesn't rush to rescue but quietly remains.

The kind that says: *I may not have known your past, but I'll walk with you into every tomorrow.*

That shoulder was not just for comfort.

It was a vow. A soft sanctuary. A sacred seat reserved in the car ride of life – the highway called life.

And as the city lights outside slowly blurred into golden smudges, as the world moved on unaware, Sagar and Riddhi sat still, heartbeats speaking in the silence between them.

They didn't talk about forever.

They didn't need to.

Because sometimes, the deepest connections aren't about declarations.

They are about quiet companionship on a long, winding road.

In that moment, they both knew,

Whatever roads lay ahead, whatever turns life might take,

they would ride on…

as co-passengers,

not just in the car…

but in each other's lives.

Even on their final ride, from *goodbye* to *forever.*

Reflection

No co-passenger rides with us forever. They enter at different stops, walk with us a while, and then move on. Some fade quietly. Others leave echoes.

We assume there's always time, for that call, that visit, that hug. Until one day, the seat beside us is empty, and it's too late.

In chasing milestones, we forget the faces beside us.

But in the end, it's not the journey we led that defines us.

It's the love that rode with us, unseen, unspoken, unforgettable.

A Note to You, Fellow Traveller

Dear Reader,

If you've made it this far, I believe you found a little bit of yourself in Sagar and Riddhi's journey. Their reflections, their silences, their search for meaning, perhaps they echoed something quietly unfolding within you. A feeling, a thought, a memory. Maybe, just maybe, you saw a glimpse of your own story playing out on this highway called life.

It doesn't matter whether you drive or not.

It doesn't matter where you began, how fast you're going, or which lane you're in.

Because this story was never about the car.

It was always about the journey - its turns, co-travellers, and the quiet moments in between.

If you chose to forgive the one who overtook you recklessly, thinking - perhaps - they were rushing into a storm of their own, the purpose of this book is met.

If you looked at a car moving slowly ahead of you and, instead of growing impatient, wondered whether the driver might be healing from a trauma you are unable to see…
the purpose of this book is met.

If, even once, you let go of an old grudge and chose to look ahead through the windshield of life, rather than fixating on the rearview mirror,
the purpose of this book is met.

If you found yourself surrounded by fog, and felt lost and uncertain, and still managed to whisper- It's okay, the road will appear eventually – even if it is ten metres at a time,
the purpose of this book is met.

If you paused to examine your blind spots, not just on the road, but in how you speak, lead, love, and live, and had the humility to course-correct,
the purpose of this book is met.

If you found yourself facing an agitated person, and instead of reacting, allowed the grace of a pause, and wondered why the person was honking, yelling, or rushing, and chose curiosity over rage and empathy over ego,
the purpose of this book is met.

If somewhere in these pages, you paused to reflect on the GPS coordinates of your life, not just where you're headed, but why you're going there,
the purpose of this book is met.

If you found yourself thinking about the handbrakes you've pulled up in life - the fear, the fatigue, the self-doubt, or the quiet scars of past setbacks - and even for a moment, considered releasing them to flow into your becoming,
the purpose of this book is met.

If a speed breaker no longer felt like a nuisance, but a grace, nudging you to notice what you've been racing past,
the purpose of this book is met.

If somewhere along these pages, you paused to notice the changing colour of the leaves when the seasons turned, and allowed yourself to turn with them,
the purpose of this book is met.

If you found your chosen lane not moving and yet chose to breathe and accept, knowing that not every decision comes with the clarity of hindsight, and what you chose back then was the best you could,
the purpose of this book is met.

If you thought about the co-passengers who will see you off to your final mile – and become more present in their lives, in word and in wonder,
the purpose of this book is met.

And above all,
Even after closing this book, if its quiet whispers stay with you - nudging you to listen more deeply, to judge less harshly,
to notice your blind spots with grace,
to sit with your fog without rushing through it,
to be more present for your fellow travellers,
and to meet life with both hands on the wheel, with reverence, patience, and love...
Then, dear traveller,

The purpose of this book is more than met.
It is lived. In you.

With gratitude and grace,

Happy navigating - this beautiful Highway called Life.

Jaskiran